KILGO

M000221008

The Bad Boys of the Cookson Hi

B

On the Cover

Top: Posse member Ray Crinklaw; headlines proclaim results of yet another shootout in the remote hills.
Center: Members of the Cookson Hills Gang – Kye Carlile, Troy Love, Jim Benge, Ford Bradshaw, Edward "Newt" Clanton, and Wilber Underhill.
Bottom: Law enforcement officers of the famous 1934 Cookson Hills raid flush out the criminals.

Contents

Preface

The story contained in these pages is a detailed description of a vicious crime and the eighteen-month long manhunt to track down the criminals involved. It details the history and crimes of a loose-knit gang of bold outlaws originally known as the Cookson Hills Gang, then the Ford Bradshaw Gang and finally the Underhill-Bradshaw Gang whose members blazed a path of robbery and murder through Oklahoma, Kansas, and Arkansas in 1932-34. It also chronicles the efforts and sacrifices of a handful of brave lawmen that tracked them down.

The description of events is taken mainly from official Federal, State, County and City records, such as, arrest, trial, appearance, bond and other court records, police reports, prison records, and US census, tax rolls, property, marriage, birth, and death records. Other sources of information were cemetery and funeral home records, old city directories, family genealogy texts, newspapers on microfilm, and magazines of the day. Oral histories were gathered by interviews, thirty-nine in total, of living participants of the story, numerous descendents of the lawmen and outlaws noted in the book, and people who lived in the area at the time. Many consented to be interviewed only if their names were not divulged.

This book came about as an offshoot of the author's and his wife's research for various stories for a weekly column on Oklahoma history for a small-town newspaper. While combing old 1930s newspaper microfilm records, the author repeatedly came across the names of Bradshaw, Clanton, Cotner, Troy Love, and "Kye" Carlile.

These names were all connected to robberies and vicious shootouts of the period in Oklahoma, Kansas, Nebraska, and Arkansas. Amazingly, the names and crimes seemed to be interconnected. This fact perked our interest and we began digging for information. What we unearthed became the basis for this book.

My wife and I spent over a year traveling hundreds of miles in four states visiting the site of every major event listed in the book. We also found and noted the burial sites of most of the characters involved in the story. Countless days were spent interviewing folks, digging through courthouse records, viewing newspapers on microfilm at libraries, and haunting museums for information.

I've tried to tell as accurate a version of events as possible. Culling through the dozens of contradictory stories told about this gang over a time span of several generations has been a formidable task. For any errors or omissions that appear in this narrative, I humbly apologize. It is a story involving many facts, dates and characters, which took place a long time ago, in what was then a very secretive segment of our nation, the famed Cookson Hills of the Ozarks. Although the names of some minor participants in the story were left out of the narrative, no names were changed. We hope you enjoy reading this tale as much as the author enjoyed writing it.

Acknowledgements

*Enter not into the path of the wicked, and go not in
the way of evil men... Proverbs 4:14*

The author lovingly dedicates this book to my wife, Naomi, a researchers dream, my Grandfather, Wilson Hopkins, who as a young man followed the exploits of John Dillinger on the radio, and passed them on to me when I was a child, and to the memories of the seven officers chronicled in this narrative, that were killed in the line of duty. Lest we forget.

A special thanks to the many residents of the Cookson Hills and others in Oklahoma, Kansas, Nebraska, and Arkansas, who generously shared information with us. Without them, this book could not have been written. I acknowledge my appreciation to Wally Waits of the Muskogee Public Library for his assistance, Lee Williams and Levi Carter for letting us stomp around their property. A hearty thanks to Aregene Clanton, Fred Gossett, John Marsh Corgan III, Donna and Clem McSpaddan, Calvin Johnson, Douglas Thomason, Paul Merritt and members of the Cannon, Powell, Lairmore, Huggins-Bradshaw, and Jackson families for their help. I also thank Mike Koch for information on the criminal career of Wilber Underhill.

About the Author

R. D. Morgan is a native of the frozen cornfields of the north. He shook the ice off his nose and joined the US Army immediately after graduating from high school, serving as a Military Police officer. After his military career, he worked several years for the federal government as an electrician in Arkansas and Missouri. Two years ago, Morgan and his wife took an early retirement and moved to Oklahoma to pursue their passion of researching and photographing people, places, and stories pertaining to 1920s and '30s history. The author got a passion from listening to his Grandfather's tales about life and culture in the Midwest during the depression years. A year ago, the couple began writing a popular weekly column in the *Haskell News* on Oklahoma history. While doing research for their column, they discovered the story of the Cookson Hills gang. Realizing the story of neither the outlaws nor the lawmen's exploits had ever fully been told they tackled the job. This book is the result of that project. The Morgans are currently active members of Oklahombres, an organization dedicated to the preservation of Oklahoma lawmen and outlaw history. They have had their stories published in the Oklahombres Journal, *Okmulgee Daily Times*, and the quarterly journal of Three Rivers Museum in Muskogee, Oklahoma.

Chapter 1

The Crime

This story begins on a lonely hilltop called Braggs Mountain in Northeast Oklahoma. On September 2, 1932, forty-eight year old Susie Sharp, the wife of E. M. Sharp, a merchant in the town of Braggs, was traveling with her family back from nearby Muskogee. They had picked up their married daughter, Mrs. Pearl Anderson, aged twenty-six, and her five-year old son, Troy, from the bus depot

Mrs. Susie Sharp and her grandson. Photo courtesy of the Muskogee-Times

where they had recently arrived from Tulsa after visiting acquaintances there. Anderson's twenty two-year old brother, Owen, the driver of the car, and Mrs. Sharp were in the front seat. Mrs. Anderson, her son, and two cousins, eighteen-year-old Edna Fulton, and Kenneth Walker, both of Braggs all sat in the rear seat.

Around 8 p.m. the car started making its way up the long grade of the mountain, seven miles southeast of Muskogee. When the automobile began to top the hill, Owen Sharp saw someone shine a flashlight directly at him. He slowed, but noticed several men, all carrying guns, on the side of the road. Fearing a robbery, the young man punched the accelerator to get past the group. Suddenly he heard popping noises and thuds that he knew were gunshots. When interviewed later, Pearl Anderson said she saw a man on the edge of the road take careful aim at the car and shoot. Owen Sharp stated that he heard his mother cry out and saw her crumple down in the seat. He braked the car; looked back, and saw none

Pearl Anderson. Photo courtesy of the Muskogee Phoenix.

of the men that had been shooting. It appeared to him his mother was gravely wounded or dead. His sister had been wounded three times in the back and was in great agony. Her five-year-old son was shot once in the leg, and the cousin, Miss Fulton was wounded in the hip. Owen and his cousin, Kenneth Walker, were not scratched in the deluge of gunfire that mainly stuck the rear of the car. At least a dozen bullets entered the vehicles interior, doing their frightful damage. He edged the car, and its grizzly cargo, with tears in his eyes, towards the filling station atop the mountain operated by Mrs. J. H. Barnett, where the wounded were unloaded. An ambulance and the County Sheriff's office were called.

****

Meanwhile, back on the side of the mountain near the ambush site, H. J. McQuowan, a salesman, living at the Muskogee YMCA, was traveling down the incline and heading home from a business trip when he also saw a man with a flashlight in the middle of the road. He stopped, and was roughly hauled out of his car at gunpoint and shoved into the ditch by five or six men. The hijackers piled into the car and began driving down the mountain at a high rate of speed, but soon lost control of the vehicle near a railroad crossing at the base of the hill, putting the car in the ditch with a broken axel.

Back up the incline, poor Mr. McQuowan, who had been treated so roughly by the gang of men, flagged down Selmar Wollard, who was traveling down the incline with a carload of Boy Scouts. Wollard was informed of the man's predicament and offered to drive him to Muskogee to the Sheriff's office. At the bottom of the hill, the carload of scouts came upon McQuowan's wrecked car. When they got out to survey the wreckage, several men rushed out of the darkness, pointing guns at the group. The hijackers piled into the second car and took off in a cloud of dust. This car, a gray Ford, was later sighted barreling through nearby Fort Gibson.

Back at the filling station, on top of the mountain, ambulances operated by the Eicholtz Funeral Home arrived from Muskogee. Strangely, when later questioned, the ambulance drivers claimed they had not noticed anything unusual as they drove up the mountainside. The victims were loaded up and the ambulances sped to Muskogee. On arrival at the Baptist Hospital, Susie Sharp was officially declared dead and Pearl, her daughter, was judged to be in critical condition. Pearl's five-year-old son was treated and released. The doctors described Edna Fulton, who was suffering from a flesh wound to the hip, as being in good condition.

Both the Muskogee and Cherokee County Sheriff's Departments responded to the scene on Braggs Mountain. The Muskogee County Sheriff's wife initially received the emergency call regarding the situation. The Sheriff was out on another call. Since there were no two-way radios then, and he could not be reached, his wife, who was known as a headstrong woman, offered to help establish roadblocks. Senior Deputy Cash Russ was finally located, nixed her idea, and headed towards Braggs.

Muskogee County Sheriff Virgil Cannon and his deputies, Marsh Corgan and Robert Ledbetter, were on a raid near Fort Gibson. Several days previously, two school-

Old Baptist Hospital circa 1930s. Photo courtesy of the Webber Falls Historical Society and Museum .

teachers had been kidnapped and their car hijacked at Warner, Oklahoma. The teachers were released but the thieves kept the car.

That morning Cherokee County officers at Barber, Oklahoma, had captured two men, Lee Hyatt and Dolph Philpot in the schoolteachers' stolen car. One of the suspects, (it was never made public as to which one), informed on their crime partners, naming Olan Scott and Bob Deerman as their cohorts in the kidnapping. Cannon and his minions completed the raid, which was successful in capturing Deerman. After transferring their prisoner to the county jail at Muskogee, Cannon was informed of the incident on Braggs Mountain. The Sheriff and his deputies immediately sped to the crime scene.

Sheriff V. S. Cannon. Photo courtesy of Claudia Chilcoat, granddaughter.

Cannon, who had been elected Muskogee County Sheriff in 1930, was born in the mountains of Northwest Arkansas in 1876. He had taught in small rural schools for several years before running for and being elected Madison County Judge in 1910. In 1917, he migrated to Northeast Oklahoma, settling near the town of Haskell, where he went into the land and finance business.

In 1929, he decided to run for the position of Muskogee County Sheriff. Within days of winning the election, the Banks of Boynton and Fort Gibson were robbed. He and his deputies quickly tracked down both sets of bank robbers. One of the bandits was the notorious Aussie Elliott, a one-time professional baseball player who made it to triple "A" before he bowed out and became a big league crook. Several other banks were robbed in the county during his two terms as Sheriff, but in every instance, the robbers were either killed or captured while he was still in office. Cannon built up a reputation as a lawman that always got his man. Unlike many county Sheriffs, he was not a deskbound politician. A lot of the credit for Cannon's efficiency was due to his good sense in appointing excellent deputies. Bob Ledbetter, a sensible man, known for his good judgment, was a fine choice for Chief Deputy. He was a man Cannon could lean heavily on. For pure muscle and grit, he had selected Marsh Corgan, the ex-Sheriff of Wagoner County, as the Chief Night Deputy. Corgan, a genuine tough guy, was a battle-hardened combat veteran of WWI.

Deputy Marsh Corgan. Photo courtesy of John Marshall Corgan III, grandson.

Cannon arrived at Braggs Mountain, about 10 p.m. Sheriff Sanders, of Cherokee County, joined him later. Together they questioned a badly shaken Owen Sharp. The young man did not recognize any of his assailants, but knew there were at least five or six men involved. The officers surveyed the assaulted vehicle, prying loose several of the spent bullets that were imbedded in the car's body. Lawmen began backtracking down the mountain road looking for clues. At the ambush site, they saw numerous shoe tracks and found several .45 caliber shell casings and one 30-30-caliber brass casing. They also ob-

The Sharp's car showing bullet holes to the front glass. Photo courtesy of the Muskogee-Times.

Owen Sharp pointing to the bullet holes. Photo courtesy of the Muskogee Phoenix.

served a dozen wax-paper sandwich wrappers lying about.

While he was at the ambush site looking for clues, Cannon was informed of a car-jacking that took place near the base of the mountain, he decided to investigate. Near the crossing of the Missouri-Pacific railroad tracks, the officers sighted the wrecked hulk of the hijacked insurance agent's car. They searched the car, finding a bag of shotgun shells, a half full jug of home brew, and observed several areas of the interior where someone had bled. Lawmen later caught up with the hijacked men and boy scouts, who had fled to a nearby farmhouse where the lawmen interviewed them.

Back at the mountaintop, Eunice Lazenby, and her friend, Loren Rhodes, of Webber Falls informed the deputies that at about 7:30 p.m. thirty minutes before the shooting, a carload of rough looking men had patronized their hamburger stand, which was attached to some sort of dancehall, located near the Barnett gas station. They stated that only one of the men entered the café, ordering twelve hamburgers wrapped in wax-paper to go, while his companions sat in the car in front of the business. Cannon, who had returned from his tour of the crime scene, went to his car and hauled in his mug books. Both women tentatively identified Luther Jolliff, a Cookson man who was currently on a $1,000 bond stemming from a federal whiskey charge, as the individual who ordered the sandwiches. Now the lawmen had a solid lead to follow.

The following day, Sheriffs Cannon and Sanders offered a $200.00 reward for information leading to the capture of the killers of Susie Sharp. Investigators were having some difficulty understanding what five or six men were doing in a wilderness area attacking cars loaded down with innocent women and children. Because of the economic hard times, there was plenty of crime in Oklahoma.

In fact, the Cookson Hills, where the crime took place, had always been noted for it's criminal element. Nevertheless, the brutality of the act shocked the public. Newspapers reported the event as far away as St. Louis.

Oklahoma's Governor, "Alfalfa" Murray, was quoted as being disgusted by the crime. The vicious killing angered many ordinary and influential people of Eastern Oklahoma. A great deal of pressure was brought to bear on local law enforcement officials to catch the killers.

A break in the case came at 6 p.m. on September 4 when Muskogee and Cherokee County deputies Grover Bishop and Marsh Corgan, along with Muskogee's Chief of Detective Ben Bolton, acting on a tip raided a house in Tahlequah and captured Luther Jolliff.

Luther Joliff. Photo courtesy of the Oklahoma Department of Corrections.

While in the course of the investigation, a hardware store operator was found in Tahlequah who stated he sold Luther Jolliff's brother, a great deal of ammo a few days past. Several witnesses came forward from the Braggs area claiming they had seen Jolliff's Model "A" (it had an unusual characteristic, the trunk lid was missing) being driven around Braggs the day of the killing. Jolliff's car was seized by officers near Keyes while being driven by his younger brother. The auto was brought to Muskogee to be viewed by the witnesses. After viewing the car, the witnesses were not certain enough to sign an official statement to the effect that it was the car in question. However, they all stated that it was similar.

******

The following day Susie Sharp, the forty-eight year old brutally murdered wife and mother of three, was remembered at her funeral at the First Christian Church in Braggs. There was a huge turnout from a community that thought a great deal of her and her family. Her husband had been a merchant in Braggs for many years. She was buried at the Green Hill Cemetery, on the northeast side of Muskogee. Her wounded daughter Pearl Anderson, could not attend although she was taken off the critical list that morning. When interviewed by officers, Pearl only remembered one assailant who stood at the side of the road, carefully aiming his weapon at the car's occupants. She stated he was tall, wore a floppy hat and bow tie. She could not identify Luther Jolliff as one of the assailant's.

That evening, a gray Ford sedan bearing license plate 273-508 was found abandoned in a cornfield in the river bottoms near Fort Gibson. The car was quickly identified as the vehicle stolen from Selmar Wollard and his carload of Boy Scouts, on Braggs Mountain and used by the killers in their flight from the crime scene.

******

Meanwhile, back at the Muskogee County Jail, Cannon's deputies began to bear down on Jolliff and the Warner kidnappers, who were all suspected by Cannon as being involved with the killers. It's safe to say interrogation techniques in 1932 were harsher than they are today. Jolliff, vehemently denied any involvement in the killing, but admitted buying twelve hamburgers at the café. He refused to divulge the names of his companions at that time.

On further investigation the police, through several unnamed sources, ascertained that Jolliff had eaten lunch the afternoon of the murder at the residence of Ben Parnell, located four miles south of the little village of Pettit, with Thomas "Kye" Carlile, Troy Love, Jim Benge, and two men known only as "Slim" and "Shorty." The three men that were identified by name were prison escapees, known outlaws, and convicted felons. After eating, the six men reportedly took target practice with a variety of weapons in their host's back yard. The authorities also found that afterwards the six men crammed into Jolliff's car, two riding in the open trunk, and headed out to do some partying.

Once officers discovered a connection between Jolliff, who was seen near the site of the murder thirty minutes before the crime and the five dangerous felons, they felt they had a good idea who the killers were. After intense questioning, one of the Warner kidnappers admitted they had been in league with the same band of criminals, being sent out to steal a car for their use in a future bank robbery. This kidnapper stated the leader of the band was "Kye" Carlile. It later came to light that during the early stages of the investigation the authorities had much more information, all backed up with sworn statements by several witnesses, than they were letting on. Prosecutors were simply being tight lipped when releasing information to the public until these witnesses could be called into open court to testify.

Lawmen first suspected the men identified, as "Slim" and "Shorty" were Cookson natives Van Ratliff and Russell King. Ratliff was suspected of kidnapping a Muskogee grocer the previous year. However, on receipt of other evidence and information from several confidential sources, authorities decided the two men were Vian native Ford Bradshaw and his partner, Eddy Clanton. The following day, the Muskogee County prosecutor, at the insistence of Sheriff Cannon, officially charged Carlile, Love, Benge, Ford Bradshaw, and Eddy Clanton with Sharp's murder.

The motivation behind including the Vian pair in the murder charge was based not only on informants' tips, but several circumstantial pieces of intelligence. First, Bradshaw was thought to have known Carlile in prison, and was suspected by authorities of participating in a Bixby, Oklahoma, bank robbery several weeks previous with him, Love, Benge and probably Van Ratliff. In addition, two men fitting the descriptions of the Vian pair had allegedly been seen in the company of Love and Carlile the week before the killing. The Vian man and his running buddy, Eddy Clanton, also matched the descriptions of the mysterious "Slim" and "Shorty" given by informants. One of Bradshaw's nicknames was "Slim" and Clanton's "Little Joe." The description Pearl Anderson gave of the tall man in the floppy hat, who took careful aim at the victims on the mountainside, also matched Bradshaw's physical characteristics. When she was shown his mug shot, she stated he looked like the man, but couldn't swear to it.

The "laws," as they were called in the Cookson Hills, had numerous theories on how the crime occurred. One theory that investigators expressed was that Jolliff had taken the killers to Braggs Mountain, bought them supper and went back to town. It stands to reason, the killers would not have shot up one car and hijacked two others to get down the mountain if Jolliff and his car had been available at the time the shooting occurred. Authorities further theorized that the group, probably intoxicated, stationed themselves on the hillside, planning to steal a car coming to or from the dancehall.

The next day, Sheriff Cannon and Muskogee Chief of Police Ed Corbin, acting on information from one of their snitches, led a contingent of officers to a location near Barber where lawmen found a burned car which was identified as similar to the one used in the Bixby robbery. When deputies walked further up the steep and heavily wooded holler, they spotted a crudely built lean to, with trash strewn about and empty shell casings on the ground, leading officers to believe they had found the killers lair. Although there were many unanswered questions about the case at that point, one fact investigators were certain of was that all the suspects came from the notorious Cookson Hills.

Chapter 2

The Cooksons and Wildcat Whiskey

The area of Oklahoma from which the murder suspects hailed was noted by the newspapers as the Cookson Hills. Most old timers generally think of the Cooksons, (which is actually a foothill section of the Ozark Mountains) as the area stretching from Tahlequah to Sallisaw in length and from the Arkansas River to the Arkansas border in width. This description actually takes in part of the Cherokee and Brushy Hills. It is a rough and heavily-forested region. The district has never held any promise as an agricultural area; the rocky tree-choked soil grows little. Due to the hilly nature of the area, only the bottomlands produced even a semblance of crops or were fit for pastureland. In some sections, if you walk ten feet off the road, you are generally swallowed up by underbrush and thick timber. There are dozens of box canyons and deep hollers in the region.

Until the 1940s and '50s, with the building and paving of a couple of roads and the damming of the Illinois River, which flows through the middle of the hills, it was an extremely isolated and inaccessible area. In 1931, there was not a paved road in Sequoyah County outside Sallisaw, the county seat. Before the coming of the tourists and fishermen in recent years, the hills were populated by mainly Indians and mixed White and Indian families. There was little industry to speak of, save a few sawmills. It was one of the most poverty-ridden places in the country. Due to the isolated nature of the Cooksons, the residents were very wary and suspicious of outsiders. They also had an undying disdain for governmental interference in their lives.

The area was dotted with small villages like Cookson, Bunch, Box, Blackgum, Barber, and Marble City. These little bergs might contain a combination general store and Post Office, a small church, and a one-room schoolhouse. Perhaps the community might feature a water-powered gristmill and a blacksmith shop. There might be five or six houses scattered around. However, most of the hill's residents lived on small farms away from any town, in houses made of stone, logs, or rough-cut sawmill lumber. The hardy souls who lived on the outlying farms were a self-sufficient and fiercely independent bunch. They raised

The original Cookson Store circa 1930s. Photo courtesy of the Lake Tenkiller Tourist Association.

hogs for meat, a cow for milk and butter, and chickens for frying and eggs. They usually had a large garden for vegetables, which women canned for future use. Hill folk grew their own tobacco, and made their medicines from nature. Many farms had small apple or peach orchards and maybe a crude sawmill. Hunting, trapping, fishing, and making moonshine whiskey were also mainstays of the residents. Until the latter '30s, many of the natives rarely traveled any further than the small villages more than once or twice a year. Trails, no better than pig or game trails, connected the little villages and isolated farms.

Before 1800, the Cooksons were the hunting domain of the Caddo and Osage Indians. Around that time, a white Indian trader named Lovely made a purchase agreement with the Osage for a 100-square-mile area of the hills, and built his own small courthouse five miles north of present day Sallisaw for the use of the anticipated influx of incoming white settlers. He named the settlement Kidron. The name was changed to Dwight Mission in 1830 after

Typical Cookson Hill homestead circa 1930s. Photo courtesy of the National Archives Digital collection.

missionaries established a school there. The Presbyterian Mission is still in operation today.

The treaty of 1817 between part of the Cherokee nation in Georgia and the US government started the western migration of that tribe to eastern Oklahoma. Cherokee Chief John Jolly established his capital, called Tahlonteeskee, near present day Gore around 1828. Nearby was the home of a Cherokee, named George Gist (Sequoyah), who invented the Cherokee alphabet.

When the remainder of the eastern part of the tribe was forced to migrate to the area, on the "Trail of Tears" in 1838-39, they established their capital at Tahlequah under Chief John Ross. Jolly's faction soon joined Ross's eastern branch forming a single united tribe with their new capital in Tahlequah (originally known as Illinois Camp Ground). Soon afterwards, numerous other tribes were forced to immigrate to this newly established Indian Territory due to President Andrew Jackson's cruel and unjust "Indian Removal Act."

In the 1830s, the white settlers were forced to vacate the area as stipulated by the treaty at the time. Several military forts were established nearby to keep the peace

Dwight Mission circa 1940. Photo courtesy of the Dwight Mission.

among the various tribes and as use as a jumping-off point for western exploration. They also acted as supply bases in support of troops being dispatched south and west during the Mexican War, and numerous Indian Campaigns. The largest and most permanent of these posts in the territory was Fort Gibson, located near present day Muskogee on the western border of the Cooksons. During the Civil War, most of the Cherokees and the neighboring Creeks sided with the Confederate cause, hoping to gain independence and just treaties from Richmond. Many Cherokees from the Cooksons fought under Brigadier General Stand Watie at the battles of Pea Ridge, Arkansas, and Honey Springs, Oklahoma, for the southern cause. Watie was the only Indian to attain the rank of General in the war. He was also the last Confederate General to surrender. During the time of the War Between the States, the Indian population suffered horribly from attacks by Union forces, lack of food, pro-Union guerrillas, and internal dissent. After the war, due to the lack of law enforcement, criminals of every stripe flooded the area for several decades.

Cherokee Nation Courthouse. Photo by Naomi Morgan.

By the 1870s, the Cherokees had created the most advanced, and educated society of all the native peoples of the time. They built a large and beautiful capital building, educational facilities, and a prison in Tahlequah. For local law enforcement dealing with Indian citizens, the tribe appointed constables, called "Lighthorsemen," in every district of their nation to keep the peace. The Cherokees had an efficient criminal justice system. On the conviction of a first crime, 50 lashes from a whip were applied to a criminal's bare back. A second offense brought a hundred lashes, and a third offense hanging. Over forty Indians were hung behind the old Cherokee Prison in Tahlequah in the latter nineteenth century.

As far as enforcement of laws applying to whites, the US Congress decreed that the area enveloping the Cooksons would be included in the Federal Jurisdiction of the Western District of Arkansas, headquartered in Fort Smith. At the end of the civil war, Judge William Story was appointed to oversee the enforcement of law in the Territory. He failed miserably because of corruption and

Prisoners at Cherokee Nation Prison. Photo courtesy of the Cherokee Nation Archives.

malfeasance. This lack of efficient law enforcement encouraged the migration to the area of many desperadoes. The old saying "no law west of Fort Smith," came from this period. In 1874, Judge Isaac Parker was named to the bench of that court to replace Story. He would serve nearly twenty years, and gain the reputation as the "Hanging Judge," due to the many death sentences he imposed. During his tenure 79 men were hung.

Parker and the Marshals under him had their work cut out. Lawlessness was rampant in the Territory. Federal marshals, such as Heck Thomas, Dave Rusk, Bill Tilghman, Paden Tolbert, and Bud Ledbetter were sent to the Cooksons to track down the bandits and outlaws that were headquartered there. Sixty-five of these Marshals were killed in the line of duty during Parker's Judgeship.

Outlaws such as Cherokee Bill and his gang hid out in box canyons in the area. The Verdigris Kid, one of Bill's

Marshal Bill Tilghman. Photo courtesy of the Okmulgee Public Library.

Judge Parker. Photo courtesy of the Fort Smith Historical Society.

partners in crime, was killed while trying to rob Tom Madden's store in Braggs, which was located on the fringes of the Cooksons, in April 1895. The Kid was the seventeenth person shot down in the Braggs area in a two-year time span. Belle Starr operated an outlaws' hideout for a price near Porum on the southern edge of the Cooksons. When Indian patriot Ned Christie was accused of killing a Marshal at Tahlequah in 1889, a crime of which he was probably innocent, he hid out in a rocky fortress in the northern part of the hills for several

Picture of Cherokee Bill on Display at the Fort Smith National Historical site. Photo by Naomi Morgan.

years. The marshals out of Fort Smith had to use dynamite to blast Christie out of his lair. The outlaw made a mad dash out of his cave and was shot down by the lawmen, then trussed up like a hog and displayed in several Arkansas cities for the enjoyment of the mainly white residents. This act caused a lot of resentment on the part of the Cherokees towards the government and the forces of law and order.

One of the more dangerous duties of the Marshals was the enforcement of the liquor laws. Ardent spirits had been outlawed in the Indian Territory and introducing liquor into the territory was a serious offense in pre-statehood days. With the advent of national prohibition, beginning with the Volstead Act in 1919 and lasting until its repeal in 1933, whiskey making became a cottage industry in the Cooksons.

The Scotch-Irish settlers of the hills, who had a long tradition of making whiskey, practiced their skill in the region. The art was passed down through the generations and was taken up by the Indian population. In the poverty-stricken hills, whiskey became a form of currency. The stuff was a natural by-product of local farms, since it was made from agriculture produce such as corn, oats, and potatoes. Home brew was also used by the hill folk medicinally. It was used for a headache, toothache, colic, sleeping potion, and a hundred and one other uses. It showed up at any community get together, barnraising, and the birth of a child, marriages, and even church gatherings. Whiskey became a socially acceptable part of the culture in the hills.

Picture of Belle Starr on display at Fort Smith National Historical Site. Photo by Naomi Morgan.

Due to the near roadless, isolated nature of the

Cooksons, where the threat from government agents trying to eradicate the making and distribution of the stuff was slim, the Cooksons were a natural for moonshiners. Uncle Sam not only did not like the proliferation of whiskey on legal and moral grounds, but wanted tax money, which was not paid on the homemade variety.

When prohibition became the national law and prices went up, a lot of local boys got into the business of making and selling "wildcat whiskey" or a strong homemade beer called "Chock," which is said to be a pretty tasty beverage if one adds dried peaches, apricots or pears into the brewing process.

With the advent of the depression, even more hill folk got into the game, for lack of another way to make a living. It is no coincidence that all of the bank robbers of the 1920s and '30s coming out of the Cooksons started their criminal careers in the bootlegging business. The hills were virtually overrun with moonshiners by the mid-twenties. Operations ranged from small family farm deals to huge

US Marshals out of Muskogee, Oklahoma, circa 1920's. Photo courtesy of Muskogee-Times.

commercial type stills. There was as many ways to brew the stuff, as there were operators.

Although many of eastern Oklahoma lawmen turned a blind eye to the crime of bootlegging, the danger to whiskey makers being spotted by Federal agents, like the legendary Joe Wilson and Don Stormont, who were pretty wily operators, wasn't taken lightly. However, even these renowned lawmen were very careful in how far they got off the beaten path in their pursuit of lawbreakers. Over the years, more than a few Federal agents walked into the Cooksons never to be seen again.

Revenuers and confiscated still. Courtesy of National Archive Digital Collection.

By the more permissive 1920s, the decade of flivers, flappers and flagpole sitters, many young people began moving to the cities looking to start a future or just find some excitement. Eking out a living in the hills, behind the plow, didn't appeal to many of the younger generation. With the advent of the radio, automobiles, and stories from returning servicemen from the war in Europe, young folks began to realize there was something out there beyond the hills. One destination for many young hill folk looking for an opportunity was Muskogee, a city lying just west of the Cooksons.

Muskogee is located near the junction of three rivers, the Verdigris, Arkansas, and Grand Neosho. By the 1920s, Muskogee was a fair sized town of 35,000 souls that boasted four hospitals, a college, and buildings that stood as tall as fourteen stories. The city's airport, Hat Box Field, was a major airport. Muskogee was also the location of one of the southwest's finest hotels, the fabulous ten-story Severs. The dream of the pioneer millionaire Captain Fredrick Severs, the posh hotel offered luxurious suites

Streets of Muskogee, circa 1930s. Photo courtesy of National Archives Digital Collections.

and a genuine French restaurant. Guests included, Will Rogers, Charles Lindbergh, Tom Mix, and Mae West. The city was a major rail hub and crossroads. It had the second largest industrial base in the eastern part of Oklahoma, bested only by Tulsa. Until the advent of the depression, jobs were plentiful, attracting many rural citizens to its bosum, who couldn't make farming pay. After prohibition became law, the town with its jobs and moneyed folk, also attracted a lot of farm boys trying to sell "home brew." Muskogee and other nearby towns also held another attraction to the more adventuresome country boys from the Cooksons, "banks to rob."

Chapter 3

The Suspects, the Lawmen, the First Manhunt

Thomas "Kye" Carlile.
Photo courtesy of
Oklahoma Department of
Corrections.

Among the main suspects in the Sharp murder case was, first and foremost the likely leader of the gang, Thomas "Kye" Carlile. Born 1901 in the Cookson Hills, he was a descendent of a large pioneer family from Cherokee County, Oklahoma. He did a hitch in the army during WWI, but after his discharge it seems he fell in with bad company. He was arrested and convicted of armed robbery on October 4, 1923, and then was sentenced to twenty-five years in the Oklahoma State Prison. He was described by prison officials as five- feet, nine-inches, 130 pounds, fair complexion, with a tattoo of a woman and a butterfly on his left shoulder, a prominent gold tooth, and a bullet scar on his left arm. After several years of good behavior, he was made a trusty at the Atoka, Oklahoma, prison farm. On May 16, 1931, he escaped and fled to Arkansas, where on October 7 he and several others robbed the First National Bank in Springdale of $5,100.

The bandits led Arkansas and Oklahoma authorities on a wild goose chase through the Cooksons for two weeks. Lawmen led by Cherokee County Sheriff Jim Sanders thought they had the crooks cornered near Barber, Oklahoma, when the posse ran onto a fresh campsite and found a sack containing $300 in silver that had been dropped by the robbers. The bandits slipped through the net, but were soon captured in Arkansas.

Carlile was again convicted of armed robbery and sentenced to seven years imprisonment. While at the Arkansas State Prison in Little Rock, he met and befriended another outlaw, Troy Love, a Pindale, Arkansas, native. In 1928, prison officials described Love, inmate #25919, as twenty-four years old, five feet- nine-inches 135 pounds, blond hair, blue eyes, and two missing lower front teeth. Records indicate that he was married to Mildred Love. The pair had produced one child, who died in infancy. Love

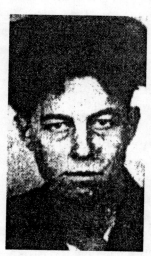

Troy Love. Photo courtesy of the Arkansas Department of Corrections.

had previously been convicted of grand larceny in Boone County, Arkansas, in 1925, and was committed to the state prison farm at Reydell for two years of hard labor. He escaped custody while working in a cotton field in April of 1926, but was recaptured in 1928 in Searcy County, Arkansas, after being spotted by local police trying to burglarize a business. A gunfight ensued in which he was shot in the right thigh and quickly surrendered. The outlaw was charged with robbery, attempted murder, and escape. He pled guilty

Jim Benge. Photo courtesy of the Muskogee-Times.

and was given a sentence of fifteen years hard labor.

Soon after Carlile and Love met, they began plotting an escape. On July 23, 1932, the pair broke out of the Little Rock facility and fled to Oklahoma's Cookson Hills. A few weeks later, the bandits were accused of robbing the Citizens Security Bank of Bixby, Oklahoma, of $1,000 with Jim Benge, Van Ratliff, and two Vian, Oklahoma, boys named Ford Bradshaw and Eddy Clanton. They settled down to hiding out in a rugged section of the Cookson Hills near Barber with other gang members and associates bringing them food and supplies while they plotted their next robbery.

A third member of the gang that the informants named was a 39-year-old Cherokee Indian, named Jim Benge, a Cookson Hills native. Benge's criminal career consisted of serving a term at the Oklahoma State Prison for manslaughter and a brief sentence on a federal whiskey charge, both in the 1920s. He was also a suspect in the 1931 Springdale, Arkansas, robbery along with Carlile. He was arrested for auto theft and suspicion of armed robbery in Newton, Missouri, in January 1932. After being held a few weeks, Benge escaped from the county jail, and went into hiding in the hills where he met up again with the Carlile bunch. He was described as six feet tall, 180 pounds with dark complexion. He reportedly was a soft-spoken man of mild disposition and even temperament. The fourth and fifth suspects in the Sharp killing were two ex-convicts, Ford Bradshaw and Edward Clanton.

Bradshaw was born seven miles northeast of Vian in the then Indian Territory in 1906. He was the son of James and Mary Bradshaw who lived on Mary's Indian allotment deep in the southern part of the Cooksons. Their home was described as a dogtrot affair with two large rooms separated by a breezeway that was constructed out of rough sawmill planks and logs. Ford was the fourth of seven children, four sons and three daughters, who were all listed on the Indian Rolls as one-eighth Cherokee.

One son was run over by a freight train at the age of fifteen in 1921. He and two other boys had been drinking home brew. After becoming groggy they laid down on the tracks to take a nap. Unfortunately, an oncoming train didn't see them until it was too late. One of the three survived. A witness, who was a child at the time, said they wrapped the Bradshaw boy's head in a sheet, put him in a homemade wood coffin and hauled him by horse drawn wagon to the Bradshaw farm for burial.

The Bradshaws were known as a hard drinking and fighting bunch. A man who grew up with them tells the story of watching one of the boys in a fistfight in town, with one of the biggest and toughest men in Vian. He said when the men hit one another it sounded like two mules kicking. He related how they beat one another senseless for thirty minutes until they both collapsed from exhaustion. Then the combatants retired to an old

Ford Bradshaw. Photo courtesy of the Muskogee-Times

barn where they commenced to drown themselves in homebrew, the best of friends.

Ford's first documented brush with the law came in 1928 when Officer John Johnson arrested him and John Rogers near Cookson, Oklahoma, on June 25, for suspicion of robbing the William's Filling Station in Muskogee with a pistol. The take was $60, some gas, and tire tubes. The pair was jailed in the Muskogee County jail where they cooled their heels until November when they were tried and convicted for the robbery. Both received five years in the State Prison in McAlester. While in prison, Bradshaw befriended Edward Clanton, a Craig County, Oklahoma, boy who had been sentenced to twenty-five years for the 1927,armed robbery of the bank at Bluejacket, Oklahoma. He also made the acquaintance of two other inmates, Wilber Underhill and Thomas "Kye" Carlile. Bradshaw was released from prison on August 11, 1931.

On the evening of October 4, 1931 Bradshaw was dropped off by two women at a gas station at Fourth and Okmulgee Streets in Muskogee, Oklahoma with a serious gunshot wound to his left side. Witnesses stated that the pair of females stayed with the injured man until the ambulance arrived, then slipped away. Bradshaw refused to cooperate with authorities, claiming he had shot himself accidentally. Detectives later backtracked his movements to an apartment at 212 West Broadway, the present day location of the Square Deal Music Shop. The place was rented to Con Deetjen, his wife

Eddy "Newt" Clanton. Photo courtesy of the Muskogee-Times

Rema, and a stepdaughter, Ruth Huggins. When questioned by Sheriff Cannon and Deputy Marsh Corgan, Rema Deetjen admitted that Ford Bradshaw was her brother. She also told the officers that she and Ford were involved in a card game that evening with Lee Markham. She said a fight erupted between the two that cumulated in gunplay. The officers noted that she was walking with a limp. She admitted that she had suffered a flesh wound to the leg in the fray. Markham was arrested, then released when neither of the two victims would testify against him in court. Muskogee authorities considered charging Rema Deetjen with obstructing justice and suspicion of running a bawdy house, but dropped the matter.

Ford Bradshaw was taken to Charity Hospital in Muskogee where surgeons performed exploratory surgery. The bullet was lodged deeply in his side, the missile breaking two ribs in its path of destruction. The young tough was kept in the hospital for some time until he recoverd. When he was well enough to leave the hospital, police had no option but to release him, having no charges to press. They filed his name away for future reference.

On December 28, Ford and another man were arrested for illegally possessing whiskey in Sallisaw; he posted a $500 bond and was released. Bradshaw's prison buddy, Eddy Clanton, was discharged from McAlester on a six-month leave of absence in early 1932. He linked up with Bradshaw at his home near Vian, making the acquaintance of his niece Ruth Huggins. The couple was soon married.

******

After the Braggs Mountain ambush, several posses made up of over one hundred men swarmed over the Cookson, Barber, and Pettit areas, where Carlile had rela-

---

tives. Roadblocks were set up on all the rough unimproved roads that snaked through the district. For two weeks, the lawmen combed the hills looking for the gunmen. Muskogee and Cherokee County Officers made numerous raids in the surrounding area resulting in the arrest of countless individuals on the charge of suspicion. Bloodhounds were brought in from the Oklahoma State Penitentiary; Cannon calling them worthless sent them back to McAlester. The Oklahoma National Guard donated some personnel, as well as Browning Automatic Rifles, tear gas, and phosphorous grenades for the posse's use.

The big break in the case occurred on September 15. There are two versions to this story, so both will be given. Bud McClain, a 28-year-old farmer from Barber, received a mysterious letter from "Kye" Carlile. It appears McClain could not read well so he asked a man to read it to him. The correspondence requested McClain to either come and

Photo of officers as they prepared to start on the manhunt for the slayers of Officer Webster Reece. They are left to right: J. A. Maupin, Sam Benge, Arthur Maupin, Cecil Speights, Muskogee County Sheriff V. S. Cannon, Cherokee County Sheriff Jim Sanders, Bob Ledbetter, C. H. Johnson and Ray Crinklaw. Photo courtesy of the Muskogee-Phoenix

get him and his partner in Troy Love's hometown of Pindale, Arkansas, or said Carlile was coming to McClain's home, wanting to be driven to a relative's house. Whatever version is correct, the result was the same. The man who read the letter for the young farmer turned the information over to the Cherokee County Sheriff's Department.

On receiving this intelligence, lawmen began observing McClain's movements. The following morning, September 16, the young farmer left, heading east in his brother's new Model "A" Roadster. That evening the roadster containing several individuals, reappeared at the McClain home near Barber.

Later that night, officers began setting set up two roadblocks, one just north, and the other south of the little village. Grover Bishop, V. S. Cannon, Marsh Corgan, and several others manned the northern roadblock. The southern barricade was manned by a posse led by Muskogee County Deputy Sheriff Webster Reece, located at the junction of the Barber cutoff and the old Cookson road, one mile east of present day Standing Rock Park. Reece, a forty-four year-old ex-banker from Braggs, had recently been appointed to his position. The other members of the roadblock were Frank Edwards, a four-year veteran of the Tahlequah police department, Tom Cook, a special deputy, and Ray Crinklaw, a man with an unusual past.

Crinklaw, a Muskogee resident, had joined the Canadian Air

Officer Crinklaw, holding a stick through his hat where a bullet had penetrated after the shootout at Standing Rock. Photo courtesy of the Muskogee-Phoenix.

Corps in 1917 during WWI. In 1918, he transferred to the American Army in France. After his service in the war, where he saw a great deal of combat, he joined the Canadian Northwest Mounted Police where he served for seven years. In 1928, he returned to Oklahoma joining the Oklahoma National Guard, as a Supply Sergeant. Crinklaw was also an auxiliary police officer, so when the posse was formed he quickly offered his services.

Deputy Reece parked his car in the middle of the curve, where the old Cookson road and the Barber cutoff merged. He manned the exposed position in front of the car, armed with a shotgun. Officers Edwards and Cook were stationed to the left side of the car armed with 30-30 rifles. Crinklaw stationed his self to the right of the car, behind a large rock; he was armed with a 30-06 Browning automatic rifle.

About 4 a.m. the posse struck pay dirt when a car's headlights were seen winding up the hill towards the roadblock carrying several passengers Crinklaw later made this statement:

"By the time the occupants of the car saw the roadblock it was too late, the narrow roadway offered no way out of the trap. Reece, standing in the road called for the car to stop. A man, (probably Troy Love who was known as a crack shot), leaped out the passenger side of the rig and started firing a rifle in our direction. Reece went down with a bullet in the abdomen. Edwards then stepped into the road firing

Officer Webster Reece. Photo courtest of the Muskogee-Times.

his rifle, and fell, shot through the mouth and shoulder. Officer Cook fired a couple of rounds then dived behind a tree stump when bullets began spattering around his feet. I raised my BAR and cut loose with a full clip into the car and the occupants. I began inserting another clip when I was struck blind by dirt and rock debris being kicked into my face by several ricocheting rounds. By the time I cleared my eyes it was over. I caught a glimpse of three men hobbling at a fast pace towards the darkness. Two of the men were holding up a third. Cook jumped into the road and fired several rounds towards the fleeing gunmen. I stepped into the road to check on my wounded comrades. Reece was in agony from a gut wound, Edwards had a horrible wound in his mouth area and his shoulder, and he was bleeding very badly."

Ray Crinklaw holding his BAR beside the bandits' car. Note the bullet holes in the glass and door. Photo courtesy of the Muskogee-Times

Crinklaw said the whole affair lasted two minutes at most. He also stated that he was certain he hit some or all of the gunmen with his automatic rifle fire. It should be noted that the story told in the Cooksons for many years concerning this ambush claims that after Crinklaw cut loose with his clip of 30-06 rounds into the suspects car he and officer Cook high tailed it into the timber to escape Troy Love's withering gunfire, allowing the suspects to easily escape the ambush site.

Officer Frank Edwards. Photo courtesy of the Muskogee-Times.

When the officers looked into the gunman's car they found an obviously dead driver, later identified as Bud McClain. The lawmen left the dead man by the road and loaded their wounded in their car. With officer Cook at the wheel, they began driving at breakneck speed to the

Close up of window of bandits' car that was in the shootout near Standing Rock. Photo courtesy of the Muskogee-Times

Tahlequah Hospital. Crinklaw's statement also told of the ride to the hospital. Crinklaw stated:

"The ride to the hospital was a journey into hell, Reece asked if he was hit bad. I said I didn't know, but I believe he knew the truth. The entrance wound of the bullet that struck him was no bigger than a dime, but the exit wound in his back was as big as softball. I had seen such wounds in combat; I knew he wouldn't make it. He must have suspected as much because he asked me to take care of his family. He also unselfishly asked me about officer Edwards' wounds and how he was holding up. Edwards, who was bleeding profusely, took his wound and pain like a man, he was very brave."

Reece died shortly after arriving at the hospital. There was nothing that could be done, the bullet, later identified as a soft nosed 30-30, had severed his aorta. Edwards was

Site of the first shootout near Standing Rock. Officers Reece and Edwards were killed here, as was Bud McClain. Arrow marks the spot where shootout occurred. Photo by Naomi Morgan.

rushed into surgery and began to stabilize.

When they received word of the gunfight, Sheriffs Cannon and Sanders immediately began forming two large posses that quickly converged on the Standing Rock Bridge area. An ambulance came along to pick up the body of the dead suspect, Bud McClain. A third posse was soon dispatched to the area, made up of Kansas State Officers and lawmen from a dozen Oklahoma Counties, as well as a contingent of Oklahoma Bureau of Investigation personal headed by C. A. Burns, sent by Governor Murray. In all, several hundred armed men began combing the hills in pursuit of the gunmen. On inspection of the car belonging to the fleeing gunmen officers found an interesting clue, a pistol with the initials D.C. scratched on the frame. Lawmen assumed the initials were that of Dick Carter, Carlile's cousin who lived in the area.

In the early afternoon of the 18th, Deputy Grover Bishop sighted Carter loaded down with groceries and supplies on the road near Pettit. Upon questioning, Carter denied that he knew the whereabouts of his cousin. Several sources claim Bishop threatened to hang Carter on the spot to get the truth out of him. He may have, Bishop, who had served in combat in WWI before joining the Sheriff's department was a rough man with rough ways. Many old time residents have described him as a cruel and violent man. He killed fourteen men in the line of duty during his career as a lawman. Whether the accusation is true, we will never

Deputy Sheriff Grover Bishop. Photo courtesy of Twin Territories Publications.

know, but Carter did admit that his cousin was hiding in a thicket with Troy Love on the old Rice Carter homestead, located about three miles northwest of present day Cherokee Landing State Park, and five miles from the site of the previous days ambush. He told Bishop early that morning the fleeing pair had forded the Illinois River and arrived at the farm of Tom Dawes, where they ate breakfast. The pair had Dawes go fetch Carter, who brought two horses to his farm for the fugitives to use in escaping the area. The plan was abandoned due to Carlile's severe condition; two bullets had struck him in the right shoulder and hand in the Standing Rock ambush. Carter admitted helping the pair get to their present hiding place at Rice Carter's farm. Love, who was only lightly wounded, refused to leave Carlile in his helpless state. His compassion cost him his life.

Bishop went to the Carter place approaching it as quietly as possible through the surrounding timber. After observing the area for an hour or so, he started seeing some activity. A story that has been told by some old- time residents of the area is, Bishop spotted two women carrying several sacks towards the thicket in question. The women suddenly stopped and headed to a hog pen where they poured out the contents of the sacks into the feed trough. The story goes on implying the women were relatives of Carlile who lived nearby. It was suspected they were taking food to the hunted men, but when they noticed Bishop, they got rid of it by feeding it to the hogs.

Bishop stated later when interviewed that he observed a man matching Troy Love's description crossing a cornfield entering the thicket. The deputy made his way back to the bank of the Illinois River several miles away where one of the large posses had been searching the timber. Once the posse numbering an estimated twenty-six members had made their way to the Carter farm, they split into three groups numbering about eight men in each, surrounding the thicket. They left one avenue, an open field to the south unguarded, hoping the gunmen would try to escape through it. The officers wanted to catch them in a classic crossfire position.

At about five that afternoon, with the temperature registering a blazing 95 degrees, at roughly the same time as Walter Reece was being lowered into his grave in Muskogee, posse leaders called for the killers to surrender. The outlaws answered with gunfire. The group of law-

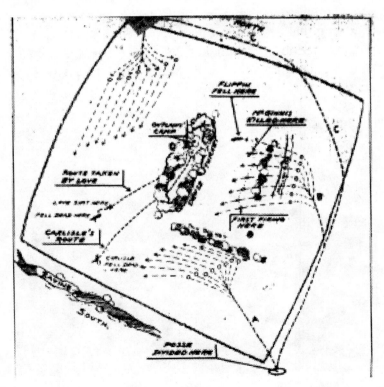

Diagram of the shootout site at the Carter farm. Courtesy of the Muskogee-Times

men and vigilantes, stationed on the northeast side of the thicket, started to slowly advance on the brushy area. Suddenly, one of the men, Andrew McGinnis, an unemployed Muskogee filling station operator with a wife and five children who had joined the posse on a fluke, foolishly ran out from behind cover and charged the thicket, screaming, "Lets go get 'em boys." He was shot through the heart, dying instantly. Another posse member, Rogers County Deputy Sheriff Hurt Flippen, suffered a severe leg wound.

On hearing the gunfire, the three groups of officers returned fire with all manner of weapons, including phosphorus grenades. A witness to the shootout told of hearing a deafening roar of gunfire which lasted several minutes, claiming that he couldn't hear for three days afterwards. Their location in the thicket must have become unbearable for the killers, because shortly after the posse fired

Carlile and Love fell near the tree line mortally wounded. Located on the old Carter homestead. Photo by Naomi Morgan.

the main volley Carlile was seen stumbling out of the open southern gap of the perimeter. He was shot down about midway between the thicket and a nearby wooded creek line, by a group of officers located near the southeast corner of the thicket. This group included Sheriff Cannon, Deputies Bishop, Corgan, and Russ, Ray Crinklaw, the hero of the Standing Rock roadblock, and several others. Soon after this, Troy Love made a run for it, and was struck repeatedly by rounds fired from the same group of lawmen. He dropped about 100 yards out through the same gap. He laid about fifty yards from his companion. The officers slowly advanced on the prone figurers lying in the tall grass. Both outlaws were obviously dead.

Several witnesses described their bodies as being literally shredded. The lawmen later stated the pair bore sev-

The old Carter farm. The arrow marks the site of the thicket, long ago cleared for pasture, where Love and Carlile were hiding. Photo by Naomi Morgan.

eral old wounds inflicted on them by their first encounter with officers at the roadblock the day before. How they recognized the wounds as old with their bodies being shredded was not explained. The posse had fired an estimated 200 rounds. When officers searched the thicket where the men had made their stand, they found bedrolls, food, and supplies. Several bullets were later found lodged in the side of the old Carter house, about an eighth of a mile from the site of the gunfight.

Several local residents, who were suspected of harboring the pair, were arrested nearby. Also apprehended was Robert Trollinger (legal name Trolinder) of Eldon,

GUN BATTLE AT COOKSON LAST SUNDAY BROUGHT DEATH TOLL TO SIX AS LONG SEARCH ENDS

Three Officers Slain, One Seriously Wounded As Warfare Ends With Slaying of "Kye" Carlile and Troy Love in Second Battle Within 36 Hours of First

Story in the Cherokee County Democrat about the shooting, calling it the bloodiest chapter in the history of the Cookson Hills that ever had been recorded.

Oklahoma, who was suspected by Cannon as being the third man who had escaped the deadly roadblock near Standing Rock the previous day. When arrested, he was observed as having glass cuts on his face and shoulder areas. Henry Carlile, the bandit's father, was held for questioning, as was Mount Cookson, a legendary area outlaw, often referred to as the "self proclaimed mayor of Cookson," a tiny village on the banks of the Illinois River, deep in the hills. The old bandit had previously served a sentence for bank robbery in the early 20s at the Oklahoma State Pen and had long been suspected by lawmen of operating a hiding place for outlaws. His son, nicknamed "Little Andy," was an escapee from the Oklahoma State Prison in Granite, where he was being confined for being an accessory to murder.

The critically wounded Deputy Flippen was transported the forty odd miles over the rough mountain roads to Muskogee's Baptist Hospital where he died the following morning from loss of blood. His wife and the Rogers County Sheriff, Dave Faulkner, were at his bedside when he expired. Flippen, one of Oklahoma's early pioneer peace officers was buried with honors at Claremore's Woodlawn Cemetery on September 21. The body of McGinnis was transported to Lasher Funeral Home, and the bodies of the outlaws ended up at the Reed Undertaking establishment in Tahlequah. The story still told in Cherokee County is that Grover Bishop threw the outlaw's bodies in the trunk of his car and

Hurt Flippen, killed in shootout. Photo courtesy of the Muskogee-Times.

hauled them to Tahlequah with their legs and arms dangling out the trunk. When Bishop reached town, he unceremoniously dumped the two men's bodies on the lawn in front of the funeral home for public viewing, until the undertaker finally came and collected them. If the story is true, and many claim it is, it was a disgusting and barbaric act on Bishop's part. That evening the two witnesses Howard Dearston and Clyde Cantner, from the Bixby bank robbery in August were brought to the funeral home where they identified the pair as two of the robbers participating in the holdup.

Deputy Walter Reece was buried in Muskogee; his wife and three small children survived him. Andrew McGinnis was buried in his hometown of Oktaha several days later. His family was left destitute. The Oklahoma Peace Officers Association gave the widows of the other officers killed in the two gunfights a $250 insurance payment, but the McGinnis family didn't qualify for the pay-

Sheriffs Sanders, Mcquillan, and Cannon. Photo courtesy of the Muskogee-Times

ment since he was only a volunteer, and not a licensed police officer. The Muskogee newspaper set up a fund for the relief of the McGinnis family, but the effort was dropped when it was found out that they would receive $100 compensation from a small private life insurance policy.

The burial of Andrew McGinnis was a bizarre affair, when his body was transported to the Oktaha cemetery it was discovered that the grave dug to receive it was in the wrong location. To remedy the oversight, his family hired four men to dig the grave again, this time in the proper spot, for ten dollars. Unfortunately, the men had gotten hold of a jug of moonshine, so naturally they decided to hold a nightlong farewell party for the deceased. By morning, the grave had been dug only about three feet deep. Being in no condition to finish the job, the quartet made due with what they had and buried the poor soul. The following morning the error was discovered and the badly hung over miscreants were forced to dig the grave to the proper proportion.

Henry Carlile and Mount Cookson were released from custody several days later. Robert Trollinger was incarcerated for several weeks before being released for lack of evidence. The elder Carlile had his son's and Troy Love's bodies taken to the Pettit Cemetery, where they were interred in a common grave. Several hundred attended the ceremony. One witness to the event stated, "The day they buried 'Kye' was the hottest day I've ever witnessed; the heat was unbearable." The Carlile family had a military stone set on their son's plot and put a rough stone slab next to it, with Love's name crudely carved on it. Bud McClain, the farmer killed by the posse at Standing Rock, was buried at the small graveyard at Barber. His widow and two small children survived him.

Around the time of Carlile's funeral, a story began spreading through the hills claiming the Susie Sharp killing had been committed by lawmen in a tragic case of misidentification. The story goes that authorities had set up a roadblock on the side of Braggs Mountain in an effort to bushwhack Carlile and his gang. When the Sharp vehicle refused to stop, lawmen mistakenly shot it to pieces. Many people could not accept the idea of Kye Carlile being accused of attacking innocent women and children, as he who had become a minor folk hero in the Cooksons, gaining a reputation as a bit of a "Robin Hood" figure. This tale is still repeated by many elderly residents of the area. Admittedly, the evidence that was made public against the named suspects at the time was slim. As far as Carlile's "Robin Hood" reputation, there is evidence that suggests he did give away some of his ill-gotten gains to needy farmers and relatives in the area over time. But if the story of police being guilty of the Sharp killing were true, it would have involved a huge cover up, implicating numerous Muskogee and Cherokee County lawmen and prosecutors. Witnesses, such as the businessman who's car was hijacked on the mountain that night, the car load of boy scouts who were later abused on the mountainside, and many others who would later testify in open court about the case, would also have had to be involved in the cover up. It presents an unlikely scenario. Another story, probably started by Grover Bishop, is that he and he alone had killed Carlile. He certainly helped, but according to police and news reports at least seven other posse men fired at the outlaw in his run for freedom.

Frank Edwards, the Tahlequah policeman from the Standing Rock roadblock who had been wounded in the mouth and shoulder, took a turn for the worse three weeks after the shooting, dying suddenly of pneumonia. He left a wife and son. Over 500 citizens attended his funeral in Tahlequah. He was buried at the city cemetery. Edwards's death was reported by the local newspaper, the *Tahlequah Citizen*, as the thirteenth violent death in Cherokee County in the past thirty days.

Elias Sharp, the widowed husband of Susie Sharp, wrote a heart-rending letter in the Tahlequah newspaper thanking the law officers for their tireless efforts in tracking down the villains, "who wrecked and ruined my life, by viciously taking the life of my loving wife and gravelly wounded my innocent child and precious grandson." He also stated, "the brave officers, who lost their lives in the two shootouts will live in my memory forever."

However, justice was not yet complete. There were three more of Susie Sharp's suspected killers, Jim Benge, Bradshaw, and Clanton still on the loose. For Sheriff Cannon, and several dozen other lawmen of Eastern Oklahoma who had witnessed the deaths of their fellow officers and saw the results of the killer's attacks on innocent women and children, justice would not be achieved until the other suspects and their associates were dead or behind bars. The manhunt for them would prove as deadly and dangerous as the one they had just completed.

Chapter 4

All in the Family, Henryetta, and the Cross Bar Hotel

The next break in the case came the following month, on October 16, 1932. About 8 p.m. a call came into the central police station in Muskogee. Doctor E. A. Welch, working at the Veterans Hospital on Honor Heights Drive, reported a car had dumped a female in her thirties in front of the hospital, and then sped away. He reported the woman was severely injured with three bullet wounds in her back, leg, and foot. Since the Veterans Hospital did not have adequate facilities for such a trauma, he called an ambu-

The VA Hospital Muskogee, Oklahoma. Photo by Naomi Morgan

lance, instructing it to take the gunshot victim to Baptist Hospital where they were better geared to treat life-threatening wounds.

Around 8:40 p.m. another call came into the police station reporting a shooting at North 39th Street, a few blocks from the VA Hospital, on Muskogee's west side. The caller would not identify himself. When police arrived at the residence that was in reality a front for a juke joint, they found an obviously dead gunshot victim on the floor of the front room. The victim was described as white, about thirty years old, five-foot, six-inches, 130 pounds, and a tattoo on his right arm bearing the initials "GLM." The home the dead man was found in belonged to "Big John" Carter, a Black man described as the proprietor of the speakeasy that offered liquor and gambling. When interviewed, Carter stated that several customers, three women and three men, had been quarreling in the establishment earlier in the evening. One of the men began yelling at a woman about being cheated out of $40 and pulled a gun. He said, a few minutes later "all hell broke loose, and bullets began flying everywhere." Carter asserted that he and a companion fled into the street for safety. He claimed not to know any of the participants by name, but they all had patronized his club in the past. When asked if one of the women was wounded in the fray, he said he believed so.

When questioned by officers at the hospital, the critically wounded woman was uncooperative. The only clue the officers had to go on was she had earlier asked the doctors about her daughter, who she said was staying at the Lindy Hotel. The police traveled to that location, which was near the railroad depot. On questioning the manager, Mrs. A. Shirley, they determined that a young woman answering the description sometimes stayed with a tenant named Stella Moody and her mother. Young Miss Moody and her companion were quickly found and under intense questioning gave their names as Ruth Huggins and Stella Mae "Boots" Moody. Both females admitted to being present at the speakeasy during the shooting. Miss Huggins claimed she did not know any of the people involved in the shooting fray. The pair was arrested as material witnesses.

Upon further questioning at the police station, Miss Moody caved in stating the individuals involved in the fracas were her boyfriend, Ford Bradshaw, and Ruth Huggins's fiancé, Eddy "Newt" Clanton. Moody also told police she didn't know the male victim. However, she stated the wounded female at the hospital was Rema Deetjen, Ford Bradshaw's sister and Miss Huggins's mother. She further told officers that she had witnessed the Deetjen woman quarrelling with the male victim. He was threatening her with a gun when suddenly Bradshaw burst into the room and shot him several times. Investagators concluded that the male victim must have also fired several rounds as he was falling to the floor, two of which struck Mrs. Deetjen, who was standing between the two antagonists. It seems that Bradshaw had also accidentally shot his sister in the foot when he released his volley at the man. The Moody girl also related how Bradshaw and Clanton had driven the three women to the nearby VA Hospital, where they unloaded the wounded Deetjen at the front door. The men then drove Moody and Huggins to the Hotel and sped off with a screech of tires into the night.

The Moody girl's mother came forward and claimed that her foolish daughter had become infatuated with Bradshaw, to the point of having his name tattooed on her right thigh beneath crossed pistols. "Boots" Moody would soon disappear, causing her family and authorities to believe her violent boyfriend had silenced her for cooperating with police. Also disappearing a short time later, never to be seen again, was John Carter, the other witness to the shooting.

The female gunshot victim, Rema Deetjen, Ford Bradshaw's older sister, was the same woman who had driven her brother, suffering with a bullet in his side, to the corner of 4th and Okmulgee Street in Muskogee the previous year, dumping the wounded Bradshaw on the roadside and fleeing. It now seems the outlaw had returned the favor. Authorities described Rema as a "tough cookie" that usually packed a pistol in her girdle.

The Muskogee Police initially had no success in identifying the dead man, until three days later when a Carthage, Missouri, man came to the station asking for assistance finding his missing son. When taken to the funeral home he quickly identified the body as his twenty-eight year old son, George L. Martin, also of Carthage. Martin, it turns out, was an escapee from the Carthage jail where he was being held in connection with the bank robberies in Jasper and Avilla, Missouri. Soon afterwards, police officially charged Ford Bradshaw and Eddy Clanton with Martin's murder. An all points bulletin was issued throughout the Midwest for the pair. It specifically warned officers that both men were armed and dangerous and Bradshaw was known to carry two guns. The two gunmen were now wanted for suspicion of murder, not only in the Martin murder, but also the Sharp killing in September. They were also wanted for questioning in the August 8 armed robbery of the Bank of Bixby, Oklahoma. Witnesses identified Love and Carlile as two of the bandits, but police also suspected Bradshaw and Clanton, as well as Jim Benge, Robert Trollinger, Van Ratliff, and possibly Fred Barker as participants in the robbery.

The pair, along with a crime partner, Charlie Cotner, were also suspects in the September 27, 1932, Vian, Oklahoma, bank robbery. Like the Bixby robbery, there were many suspects in this heist, although if local lore has any bearing, they were the guilty party. A lot of old-timers in the Cooksons today insist the trio pulled the Vian job. If Bradshaw was involved, it was the second time a family member had held up the bank. Jim Bradshaw, the boy's father, had been convicted of robbing the institution in 1920. Whoever hit the bank struck paydirt; the take was over $6,000 of cotton money. Possibly Bradshaw was trying to walk in his daddy's footsteps. On October 21 Tulsa police sighted Bradshaw's car on the city's east side and began a high-speed chase, but the vehicle soon out ran the pursuing patrol cars.

On November 1 in Muskogee County District Court, two of the four hijackers charged in the kidnapping and

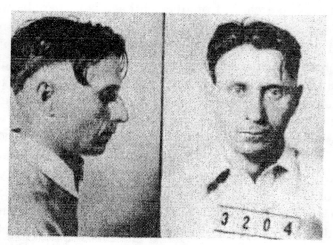

Fred Barker's mug shots. Photo courtesy of the Springfield News and Leader.

auto theft involving the two schoolteachers near Warner had their day in court. They were both sentenced to seven years hard labor in Oklahoma's Granite prison. One of the men had previously admitted they were stealing the car for the suspects in the killing of Susie Sharp to use in an upcoming bank robbery. A third suspect, Bob Deerman, was released for lack of evidence.

******

Shortly after lunchtime, November 7, 1932, three men entered the American Exchange Bank of Henryetta, Oklahoma. One man was stationed just inside the main entrance bearing a sawed off-shotgun, while the other two walked calmly into the lobby of the bank. Only two employees, Al Diamond and T. T. Tarpley, were on duty at the time. Tarpley was at the cashier cage and Diamond manned a posting machine. Neither of the bankers noticed a thing

The Bixby Bank today. Photo by Naomi Morgan.

until someone stuck a pistol into Diamond's back, calling for him to "get em up" in a gruff manner. He was handed a sack and told to "fill it up." Tarpley was ordered to sit on the floor and not move. The bandit doing all the talking stated they would "as soon kill you as anyone." Mr. Diamond and the lead bandit went into the vault and gathered up nearly $12,000 in cash, while the other two bandits manned the lobby and front door respectively. About this time Wilburn Harris, a young man who worked for the *Henryetta News*, strode into the bank lobby. The outlaw manning the front door armed with the shotgun, whom witnesses described as an Indian, ordered Harris to stand against the wall and be still. After gathering up the cash in the vault, the lead bandit ordered Tarpley and Diamond to walk out the front door in front of the robbers and get into a new maroon Chevrolet parked in front of the bank. They allowed young Harris to remain in the bank, admonishing

American National Exchange circa around 1940. Photo courtesy of Henryetta Historical Society.

him to stay sitting on the floor and be quite for ten minutes or else they would return someday and kill him. After walking to the car, Tarpley was forced to sit in the back seat between two of the desperodoes and Diamond was directed to hop on the left running board of the getaway car, and told to hang on tight. After driving east on Main Street for two blocks and noticing there was no public outcry, the bandits let their captives out in front of the Blaine Theatre and admonished them not to spread the alarm for ten minutes. The bandits sped off in an easterly direction.

Meanwhile, young Harris ran to the nearby Kroger Grocery store and called the Police. On arrival at the bank, several officers rounded up the employees and witnesses while others raced out of town trying to catch up with the bandits, but to no avail. Okmulgee County Sheriff Jim Stormont was contacted and quickly arrived at the scene of the robbery. He sent deputies to set up roadblocks at

Inside the American National Exchange Bank circa 1920s. Photo courtesy of the Okmulgee Public Library.

numerous crossroads and bridges throughout the area.

The Sheriff's department was very familiar with the drill. Several area banks had been robbed in the county in the past year. On September 8, 1931 the notorious, "Pretty Boy" Floyd hit the nearby Morris State Bank. Later the same week, the Bank of Hitchita was knocked off. In December of that year, Floyd again robbed the Morris bank. On May 29, 1932 the incredibly unlucky Morris State Bank was robbed a third time. This time a vicious gunfight erupted between the local citizens who had armed themselves and the robbers. The chief cashier, Clara Aggas, was shot in the face and arm. One of the bandits was killed on the spot and several bystanders wounded.

Hard times produced by the great depression was very evident in the county. The economic downturn and the responding drop in cotton prices, the mainstay crop of the area, produced enough poverty so that the crimes of rob-

The old Blaine Theater circa around the time of the robbery. Photo courtesy of the Henryetta Historical Society.

bery and theft had dramatically increased in this the so-called cruelest year of the deppression. Stormont had witnessed a decline in assistance that was offered by the citizens in helping solve the crime of bank robbery. With the stock market crash and the collapse of several small banks in the area in 1930 and '31, many citizens lost their life savings. Feelings of good will towards the banks were at an all-time low.

Back at the bank, witnesses as they usually do gave several contradicting descriptions of the robbers. However, one thing they agreed on was that they were seasoned pros; this certainly had not been their first bank robbery. When asked if they thought the notorious "Pretty Boy" Floyd, the archenemy of all Oklahoma bankers, was the villain that had robbed the bank. Clerks Tarpley and Diamond thought not, but several residents spread the news all over town that the clever Floyd was the guilty party. Even the Sheriff concluded that one of the robbers was the slippery bandit. This confusion would come back to haunt the investigation in the future.

On the evening of November 16, 1932, the mystery started to unravel. In nearby Nuyaka, a farmer named Alf Mays reported the shooting of three persons at his home earlier that day. When lawmen arrived, they found a pair of brothers, Bill and Bob Henson, and their uncle, Lee Sharp, all suffering from bullet wounds. Bill Henson's wife had also been severely beaten. Alf Mays and his wife Laura stated the attacker had been their son-in-law, John Lindsey, who had been distraught over his wife, the Mays' daughter, leaving him, supposedly for another man. The pair claimed that a very intoxicated Lindsey had come to their home earlier that afternoon threatening his family with violence. Mays stated that Lindsey wanted to talk to the Henson brothers, who were his brothers-in-law. Lindsey and the Henson brothers were all married to Alf Mays' daughters. The brothers were phoned and asked to come to the Mays' home to calm the irate Lindsey, which they agreed to do.

On questioning, the Hensons stated that on their arrival at the Mays's farm in Nuyaka, Lindsey shot both of them and then turned the gun on their uncle, Lee Sharp, who had come along for the ride. Lindsey then chased down Bill Henson's wife who he commenced to beat severely in the hayloft of the barn. The Doctors at the Okmulgee City Hospital asserted that none of the victims were suffering from life-threatening injuries. Okumulgee County Sheriff Jim Stormont had an APB and an arrest warrant issued for Lindsey. Posses were formed and began combing the Nuyuka area with bloodhounds.

On Wednesday, November 18, Constable Max Shelton sighted a man near a creek outside the little village. Other officers were called in, surrounding the area. The man was again sighted, this time entering a nearby thicket. The leader of the posse called for the suspect to come out with his hands up and identify himself, which he did. It was indeed the wanted suspect, John Lindsey. Officers described the man as being in a state of intoxication. No firearms were found at the location. Lindsey was transported to the Okmulgee County jail, where he began making a rambling statement implicating him and several others in various crimes. He admitted shooting the three men, but stated that his motivation involved being cheated out of his share of the proceeds of the recent Henryetta bank robbery. This immediately got the attention of the interrogating officers, who quickly sent for the District Attorney and a stenographer.

The tale John Lindsey related was one of self-incrimination. He stated that on November 6, the day before the bank robbery, three men who were acquaintances of his wife arrived at his father-in-law's farm. The men were seeking someone to case the Henryetta bank and wanted to use the Mays farm as a place to lie low for a day or so after they robbed the bank. Lindsey claimed his wife and her father, along with a friend named Jones, agreed to the arrangement for a price. The following morning Lindsey's wife allegedly drove to the bank and scouted out the setup there. She returned about 10 a.m. with the information the three men requested. Lindsey identified the men as Ford Bradshaw, Eddy "Newt" Clanton, and Jim Benge.

Lindsey stated the three left Nuyaka about 11 a.m. and retuned about 1 p.m. Jones opened the gate for the bandits, who were driving a late model maroon Chevy. They drove behind Mays' chicken house and parked the car where it couldn't be seen from the road. Bradshaw handed Jones the car's license plate and asked him to bury it, he pulled out a spare plate from the trunk and attached it to the getaway vehicle. He then asserted that the three bandits went into the farmhouse where the spoils from the robbery were divided up. Lindsey, Mays, and Jones were given $50 apiece and another $1,200 was left with the Mays to be split up later amongst the three men.

Lindsey claimed that after nearly two weeks had lapsed without getting his cut of the $1,200, he became upset and decided to get his slice of the pie, one way or another. He went to his father-in-law's place armed and meaning business the morning of the shootings. He also stated that on arriving and confronting old man Mays about the money, Mays claimed the Henson brothers processed it. Lindsey told officers when the Henson brothers arrived at the Mays farm they had tried to kill him, so he shot them in self-defense.

When questioned, the Henson and Mays family disputed Lindsey's statement, and stuck with their original story. When lawmen searched the Mays farm, the buried car plate was found as well as several money wrappers which were stamped the "American Exchange Bank of Henryetta." Mays and Jones were charged with harboring fugitives from justice. Lindsey was charged with attempted murder and harboring. Warrants were issued for the arrest of Ford Bradshaw, Ed Clanton, and Jim Benge for bank robbery.

******

Meanwhile the Bradshaw home near present day Sycamore, Oklahoma, northeast of Vian, had become after "Kye" Carlile's death the headquarters of the newly formed Cookson Hills gang. Bradshaw's crew swelled and shrank at times, but the core element of the gang for the years 1932-34 was made up of Ford Bradshaw (born in 1906), and his younger brother Tom (who was nicknamed "Skeet" and was born in 1910), Eddy Clanton, Charlie and Hunter Cotner, Jim Benge and the notorious Eno brothers, Clarence and Otis. Mount Cookson, Robert Trollinger, and a half dozen others floated in and out of the gang. They were a loose knit group that at times seemed very organized and at other times not.

Ford's sister, Clara "Gypsy" Bradshaw born in 1915, was married to Otis Eno. Another sister Willi, nicknamed "Rema," and born in 1899, was every bit as rough as her three brothers. She was suspected of and questioned several times for running so called "bawdy houses" over the years that offered illegal gambling and safe harbor for criminals on the run. She was also a suspect in the G. L. Martin murder investigation. Eddy Clanton was married to Rema's daughter, Mary Ruth. The elder brother, Kerman, seems not to have taken an active role in his brother's illegal activities, but was known by as a tough character. A story commonly told about him was that Kerman liked to hunt rattlesnakes. Once he caught a rattler measuring over six feet when stretched out. When the snake accidentally bit him, he refused medical treatment. His only noticeable reaction was to stretch out on the couch for a few hours. Witnesses say he turned a mite pale, but survived no worse for the wear.

The Bradshaws were a close-knit family, and by all accounts loved their home brew, or "wildcat whiskey" so commonly found and made in those days. All indications are they didn't make a lot of whiskey, but certainly transported and sold a great deal of the illegal substance early in their criminal careers. Old timers remember the father, Jim Bradshaw, a blacksmith by trade, as an intelligent and semi-respected man in the Vian area, though there are many stories of him being the planner of numerous robberies and having his hand in the local moonshine businesses. He had previously served eighteen months of a five-year term in Oklahoma State Prison for the robbery of the Bank of Vian in 1920.

The family moved from Missouri to Vian in 1903. They later settled in a heavily-wooded and hilly section of the Cooksons six miles south of Dwight Mission in 1906, on a Cherokee allotment granted to the family through the mother's pedigree. They built a large cabin about a hundred yards from the site of the old Sycamore schoolhouse. The boys grew up in rough country, under poor cirmumstances, as noted by the fact they had lost some of their land in 1923 and 1927 for failure to pay their property taxes. After the state seized the land for back taxes, it was bought by a wealthy land company owned by a bank in Florida which had come through the country picking up bargains by buying out poor farmers who couldn't make ends meet for dime on the dollar prices. The father, Jim Bradshaw, also foolishly mortgaged his children's Indian allotment land repeatedly, putting his wife and children's birthright in constant danger if the bank unexpectedly called the note. It is no wonder the Bradshaws disliked banks, however they could blame their father for some of their problems in that direction.

Prison records, newspapers, and old timers described Ford Bradshaw as being six-foot-one-inch, 160 pounds, with sandy hair, and blue eyes. He was also noted as intelligent, and was a notorious skirt chaser who had a good sense of humor and a propensity for violence. Ford was the more outgoing of the brothers. Tom "Skeet" Bradshaw was six-foot-two-inches, 150 pounds, with chestnut hair and blue eyes. He was evidently the quiet type, unless riled or intoxicated. He also greatly enjoyed the company of the opposite sex.

One would think their neighbors would dislike and fear the gang members, but the country and the times they lived in must be considered. With the collapse of the stock market in 1929, and the bottom falling out of the cotton market, times were tougher in the Hills than before, and that is saying a lot. With the droughts of 1930 and '32, gardens burned up and cows and wells went dry. Livestock had to be driven miles to water. Food became scarce. Even "Hoover Hogs," local slang for squirrels and rabbits during President Hoover's term in office, became as hard to find as jobs. Oklahoma as a state was only two decades old and was ill prepared or organized to handle a calamity the size of the deppression. Federal assistance from Washington was slow to come. Unemployment hit forty percent in Eastern Oklahoma in 1933. Few generations of Americans suffered as much as those who lived through the "dirty thirties" in Oklahoma.

After each of their robberies, the Bradshaws put on huge community feasts which lasted several days. Food and drink was plentiful. Some of the robbery proceeds was always spread throughout the community. Most folks, struggling to feed their families, wouldn't turn down a few dollars in help from some local boys who to their way of thinking only hurt banks and rich outsiders with their doings. It is not hard to understand why the poor, but proud people of the Cooksons, began to look at these bandits as "Robin Hood" figures. Although their motivation was not always pure, many of the Cookson bandits of the '30s did take from the rich and give to the poor.

Another family close to the Bradshaws was the Cotners. Charley (nicknamed "Cotton"), born in 1900, was the oldest. He was a partner of Ford Bradshaw and a friend of Charles "Pretty Boy" Floyd from nearby Akins, Oklahoma. He was described as a tough ex-con with a photographic memory. Cotner had shot a man in a bank robbery in Fayetteville, Arkansas, in 1924. He was arrested and convicted of robbery and attempted murder on June 30, 1924, in Washington County. He entered the Arkansas State Pen on July 10 as inmate #21524. He was paroled in 1930 to Oklahoma, and went to work for a man named J. F. Pennington. He and his brother, Hunter, were involved with the Bradshaws since childhood. The boys had two sisters, a redhead named Blanche, who was said to have been at one time romantically involved with Ford Bradshaw and another sister, who married one of the Bradshaw cousins.

******

Nothing had been heard from the Bradshaws for over a month when on December 12, 1932, a garage owner in Miami, Oklahoma, called Sheriff John York reporting a pair of suspicious characters who had wrecked their car, a brand new Plymouth, on an ice covered road and had hired him to tow it to his garage for repairs. The pair had given the garage owner $20 on deposit and told him to repair the car. They stated that they were hiring a taxi to go on to Chelsea, about thirty miles to the southwest. They also stated they would return for the car in a few days. On inspection of the wrecked auto, the owner not only noticed a burst radiator, but numerous boxes of rifle and pistol ammunition in the backseat, and an armored vest in the trunk. He immediately reported his findings to local authorities.

After being notified, Craig County Sheriff York and two carloads of deputies met the taxi hired by the suspects on Route 66 near the town of Vinita, about halfway to the pair's destination in Chelsea. The lawmen surrounded the car, while the Sheriff armed with a Thompson machine gun, yanked open the front door and demanded the men "put em up." The pair surrendered with no resistance. The suspects, dressed in fine suits and silk ties, were cuffed

Craig County Sheriff York. Photo courtesy of Craig County Sheriff's Department.

and transported back to the Craig County jail. The duo gave their names as Johnson and Smith, claiming to be traveling salesmen. The lawmen didn't buy the idea of salesmen needing bulletproof vests and boxes of pistol ammunition, or the fact that both men were armed with Colt .45 caliber automatic pistols in their belts when arrested. Another incriminating factor was that the men were carrying $1,500 in cash when searched, a very unusual occurrence in the depths of the depression. Rent receipts and other documents found on the pair and in their car showed that they had been living in a small flat at 1108 Harrison Avenue in Springfield, Missouri, for the past month. On contacting authorities in Missouri, Miami officials were informed that the pair had been under observation for the past two weeks. The police in Springfield suspected they were bootleggers. After reviewing his wanted posters, the Sheriff figured the pair matched the description of the Bradshaw brothers.

Miami officers contacted authorities in Okmulgee and Muskogee Counties informing them of their catch. Okmulgee County Sheriff Stormont responded by gathering the witnesses from the bank robbery in Henryetta and driving them to Miami. Bank clerks, Diamond and Turley, identified Ford Bradshaw as the leader of the gang who had robbed the bank. "Skeet" could not be identified as one of the bandits, but was charged with carrying a concealed weapon by the Craig County prosecutor. Officers speculated that the brothers were heading towards a meeting with their partner, Newt Clanton, who had relatives living near Chelsea.

Muskogee County officials also showed up in Miami, but because of problems they were encountering in rounding up witnesses, they conceded to let Okmulgee County try Ford Bradshaw first. He had two murder warrants against him in Muskogee, but of the four witnesses in the Martin killing, Big John Carter and "Boots" Moody had disappeared, while Bradshaw's sister and niece weren't talking. In the Sharp murder case, no one was willing to testify against Bradshaw. The one witness who had been somewhat coopertive, Luther Jolliff, had been released on a $2,000 bond. He jumped bail and melted back into the Cooksons, not being seen for several months.

Ford Bradshaw was transported back to Okmulgee that night and immediately arraigned in the courtroom of Justice of the Peace R. E. Jenniss, where he pled not guilty. Jim Bradshaw, the defendant's father, hired Harry Pitchford, a one-time Sequoyah county prosecutor turned defense attorney, to represent the outlaw. Bond was denied. The selection of Pitchford turned out to be fortuitous for the bandit; he was an excellent attorney.

Chapter 5

The Toll Bridge, Wilber and Company

With the Bradshaws safely tucked away in two separate county jails, little was heard from the other members of the gang who remained at large. Law enforcement officials of the Eastern part of Oklahoma had come to the conclusion that they were lying low, or trying to come up with a plan to spring their incarcerated companions.

About six weeks after the Bradshaws capture, the gang devised a plan to bring in some funds, one that did not require much thinking. On the evening of February 1, 1933, Dr. and Mrs. J. L. Post were driving about five miles north of Webber Falls toward Muskogee, approaching a small bridge when the physician noticed a car parked across the road. Naturally, the good doctor stopped, figuring there had been a wreck or an emergency of some sort. He later mused that he thought someone could use his services. This was not the case; several armed men quickly surrounded the car and ordered him to drive down a small lane to the right of the main road. The physician did what he was told while observing another car already parked on the lane. When he stopped the vehicle, he was approached by what he described as a big Indian. The man demanded his money and valuables. After noticing the man was heavily armed, he complied with his demands to the tune of over $100 in cash, a watch valued at $80, and his wife's jewelry, worth about $400. He stated that the occupants of the car in front of him on the lane were also forking over their valuables. He later said the bandits stopped several cars in a twenty-minute period. "They had a real assembly line of robbery going on, like they were operating a toll road," the Doctor chuckled.

When the physician got to Muskogee he reported the robbery to the Sheriff's office, which was already aware of the bold robberies. He and Mrs. Post identified Jim Benge and Eddy Clanton from mug books as two of the bandits. Officers rushed to Webber Falls in pursuit of the outlaws, but drew a blank.

******

In mid-February, Alf Mays, from whose farm the gang had allegedly launched their attack on the Henryetta Bank was brought to trial on a charge of harboring the bandits. A jury heard the prosecutor's evidence which was rebutted by a firm denial of any involvement of the crime by

The Okmulgee County courthouse circa 1930s. Photo courtesy of the Okmulgee Public Library.

the defendant. On March 1, 1933, the jury acquitted him of all charges. The Judge and the Sheriff were dumbfounded. It seemed that the hatred of banks and bankers was stronger than any distaste for bank robbers. The Okmulgee area had been hard hit by the depression and feelings against the rich, especially bankers, was running high. Bradshaw's trial was put off until the next court term. The District Attorney hoped that a different jury pool could be collected then, thus proving that class warfare was certainly alive and well in Okmulgee County in the dark days of the depression.

On the afternoon of February 27, while Ford Bradshaw was awaiting trial, three men robbed the Chetopa State Bank in Kansas for $1,300. Two witnesses identified from mug books one of the robbers as Ford's brother, "Skeet," who had been released by Miami authorities the previous week. A warrant was issued for his arrest.

When Ford Bradshaw's case was finally called on May 26, it was a controversial affair. Attorney Pitchford accused the court clerk and newly-elected Sheriff John Lenox of unlawfully picking a prejudiced jury pool. He also claimed the Sheriff was prejudiced against his client. He pointed out the fact that the lawman had told numerous citizens around town that Bradshaw was guilty. Judge Mark Bozarth overruled the attorney and impaneled the

Judge Bozarth of Okmulgee County who presided at Bradshaw's trial. Photo courtesy of the Okmulgee Public Library.

jury. John Lindsey, the man who went on the shooting spree the previous November claiming he was cheated out of his cut of the robbery procceds, was the first to testify. Lindsey had to be transported from the prison facility at Granite, Oklahoma, where he was serving a twenty-year term for the attempted murder of the Henson brothers. His testimony implicated Bradshaw, Clanton, and Benge as the alleged robbers. When the two bankers took the stand, they also identified Bradshaw as being present at the robbery.

Attorney Pitchford countered with the testimony of numerous citizens including the newspaper editor and ex-Sheriff Stormount, all of whom immediately after the crime stated the bandits had been Charley Floyd and his sidekick in crime, George Birdwell. The personal dislike for one another by the attorney and Sheriff Lenox was apparent throughout the trial. Defendant Bradshaw did not testify in his own defense. The case went to the jury on May 27; it had been all in all a brief trial. After twenty minutes of deliberation the jury acquitted Bradshaw of all charges. The local newspaper reported spectators in the courtroom burst into applause when the verdict was announced.

Muskogee County officials, shocked by the verdict, immediately put a retainer on Bradshaw. They stated that they would try him for both the Martin and Sharp murders. On the morning of May 30, Bradshaw was transported to the Muskogee County jail for safekeeping. County attorneys began scrambling in an effort to find witnesses who would testify against the bandit. At the same time as Bradshaw was being transporting to the Muskogee County jail, an event that would have a bearing on the rest of this story was transpiring in northern Kansas.

******

On Memorial Day 1933, at the Kansas State Prison in Lansing, eleven desperate convicts armed with guns smuggled in from the outside overpowered and captured the Warden and several guards near the prison's main gate. The Warden, Kirk Prather, ordered the tower guards to open the gates and the convicts commandeered a car, speeding off in a southerly direction. They soon split up into several smaller groups. One of the groups of escapees was made up of several notorious criminals including Wilber Underhill, Harvey Bailey, Ed Davis, Frank Sawyer, and Jim Clark. Bailey, when interviewed in the 1970s by author L. L. Edge, stated the group's destination was the Cooksons, where they felt they would be safe from the clutches of the law.

Warden Kirk Prather. Photo courtesy of the Kansas Department of Corrections

One of the leaders in the break, Wilbur Underhill, was a man with a long and violent criminal

Wilber Underhill. Photo courtesy of the Okmulgee-Times

Five of the escapees. TOP: Jim Clark, Harvey Bailey, and Ed Davis. BOTTOM: Bob Brady, and Frank Sawyer. Photos courtesy of the Kansas Department of Corrections.

Kansas State Prison circa 1930s. Photo courtesy of the Codding family.

past. Raised in the Joplin-Galena lead mining district, he appears to have started his life in crime by selling bootleg whiskey to the tough miners. He and his two brothers were all career criminals. In 1920, he had been arrested for attempted robbery and sentenced to two years in the Missouri State Prison. After his release he was soon arrested again and convicted for first-degree robbery, and was given five more years at the same institution. When released the second time, he left the state traveling to Oklahoma where he robbed and shot a man in the small town of Picher. In 1926, he partnered up with a small-time thief named Ike Akins. On Christmas day the pair robbed a drug store in Okmulgee, killing the clerk, nineteen year-old George Fee, during the robbery. On January 7, 1927, the pair was apprehended by Tulsa Detectives and transported back to Okmulgee to stand trial.

On the 30th of that month, the duo, along with two other inmates sawed through their cell bars and climbed out on the ledge of the fourth floor jail. Using blankets tied together as a rope, the men gained their freedom. Akins was soon captured in Lamar, Missouri. Okmulgee County Sheriff John Russell and his Chief Deputy, Mark Lairmore, a pair of rugged Texas born cowboys turned lawmen, were sent to retrieve him. On the

Deputy Mark Lairmore. Photo courtesy of John Lairmore, son.

way back to Okmulgee, an intense thunder burst came up and the officers had to pull off the road near Mounds, Oklahoma, to wipe their windshield. After the car was stopped and the officers were busy, Akins made a break out the back seat, running towards a cotton field. Lairmore hollered a warning and Russell turned and shot Akins three times, killing him. This was not the first time Russell had shot an escaping suspect. He and Lairmore shot at least a dozen men in the line of duty during their legendary careers.

Meanwhile, Underhill took advantage of his new found freedom by robbing and plundering at will. In his next act of depravity he shot and killed a citizen named Ed O'Neal who was helping a local police officer put handcuffs on the outlaw after he had been arrested for robbing a theatre in Picher, Oklahoma, of $52. He escaped custody, but was finally run down by lawmen in Panama, Oklahoma, on March 20, 1927. The outlaw had been spending the night with a woman he claimed was his wife in a local hotel. When Underhill tried to leave the Hotel the following morning, officers met him. When ordered to put his hands in the air, he responded by reaching for his back pocket. Lawmen shot him in the arm and thigh. The newspapers reported he was also given a good thrashing by officers later that night at the jail.

Sheriff John Russell. Photo courtesy of John Russell Jr and the Okmulgee Public Library.

He was soon hauled back to Okmulgee for a second time and lodged in the county jail under heavy guard. On June 3, a jury convicted Underhill of the murder of George Fee. He was given a life sentence at the Oklahoma State Prison. Sheriffs Lairmore and Russell transported the hoodlum to the Penitentiary. While in route the killer tried to slip out of his handcuffs and the lawmen responded by informing him that if he tried that again he would get the same as his partner Akins got. There was no more trouble out of Wilber.

On July 14, 1931, while working on a prison road gang, Underhill escaped custody, this time fleeing towards Kansas where he connected with his nephew, Frank Underhill, a want-a-be tough guy. On August 1, the pair robbed a movie theatre in Coffeyville, Kansas. On the evening of August 13, the duo hit a gas station near Witchita, where the take was a whopping $14.68. The pair then checked into a downtown hotel. The next morning, Underhill shot and killed Wichita policeman Merle Colver, who was checking identifications of residents staying at the hotel. He was captured later that day. Underhill, who would be described as a psychopath today, was again convicted of murder and sentenced to life, this time at the Kansas State Prison. Wilber was

Wilber Underhill's gun that was used to shoot and kill Police Officer Merle Colver. The gun is on display at the Davis Gun Museum. Photo by Naomi Morgan.

certainly a walking billboard advertisement for pro- death penalty advocates.

*****

Of the other escapees in Underhill's group, Harvey Bailey was thought to be the most successful bank robber living. It was suspected that he had a hand in the 1930 robbery of the Lincoln National Bank in Nebraska, which netted the bandits $2.7 million dollars in cash and bonds. He had also been involved in numerous other robberies in the Midwest through out the 1920s. Unlike Underhill, he was profiled as nonviolent and a real pro.

The rest of the group was made up of Ed Davis, who was doing life for murder, Frank Sawyer who had committed several robberies with Harvey Bailey, Bob Brady, and Jim Clark, an Oklahoman, who had once been convicted for stealing a cow in his hometown of Muskogee.

Towards evening on May 30, Underhill and his fellow escapees released the Warden and the other hostages near the Oklahoma border. The next day the group was suspected of murdering constable, Otto Drake, in Chetopa, Kansas, then robbing a filling station in Miami, Oklahoma.

******

Bank of Chelsea, Oklahoma Photo by Naomi Morgan.

The following day, six well-dressed men driving a new car robbed the Bank of Chelsea, Oklahoma. Four of the bandits entered the bank while two stood guard at the front door armed with sawed-off shotguns. An elderly Rogers County man, who witnessed the event as a child and was standing near the front of the bank at the time of the robbery, stated one of the bandits told him to "get your ass out of the way."

When informed of the ongoing robbery, city policemen Tom Dean and Ed Chiles took cover in a nearby hardware store and opened fire on the two bandits standing in front of the financial institution. After a sharp exchange of fire, the police backed off, fleeing deeper into the building. The bandits finished their business and drove out of town at a rapid pace. The two Chelsea officers, who were joined by Deputy Sheriff Bob Walters and several other citizens, gave chase. One of the posses' chase cars, driven by Clarence Merriott of Chelsea, was hit in the radiator by flying bullets causing the vehicle to crash into a ditch. The bandits fled south on US 66. The pursuing lawmen soon lost sight of the fleeing robbers. A carload of unsuspecting businessmen driving north on Route 66 was riddled with bullets as it passed the robber's car on the highway. Miraculously the estimated fifty bullets fired that day injured no one.

Although several witnesses came forward accusing Wilber Underhill and his fellow escapees of robbing the bank, lawmen disagreed. They suspected Cookson Hill gang members, Clarence and Otis Eno, along with Eddy Clanton and several Nowata County men as being the culprits in the robbery.

******

During the month of July, Underhill and his fellow escapees, minus Frank Sawyer who tried to go solo and was soon captured, robbed the Banks of Clinton, Oklahoma, and Canton, Kansas. On August 9 Underhill, Bailey, Clark, and Bob Brady allegedly robbed the Peoples National Bank of Kingfisher, Oklahoma, for $6,024. Underhill and several of his companions had been using a cabin near Titanic, Oklahoma, on the northern edge of the Cooksons as a base of operations during the robbery spree.

******

Back at the Muskogee County Courthouse, legal maneuvering was going on in the case of The State of Oklahoma vs. Ford Bradshaw. His attorney, Harry Pitchford, had come to the conclusion that the state couldn't find any witnesses to testify against his client and were holding him in jail till some could be found. Pitchford, a slick and gutsy lawyer, knew that in the G. L. Martin murder case (the gambler who Ford had allegedly killed) there was a complete lack of witnesses. The chief witness and owner of the speakeasy, John Carter, had disappeared. Sheriff Cannon was on record saying he suspected Bradshaw had silenced him shortly after the crime. He told newspapers that Carter would probably be found floating in the Illinois River someday. Also missing was Bradshaw's girlfriend, Stella "Boots" Moody. Police also suspected foul play in her disappearance. The other witnesses, Bradshaw's sister Rema and niece Ruth Clanton, wife of gang member Eddy Clanton, were not trusted by the District Attorney to give any evidence against the outlaw. The law was in a bind in the case.

In the Sharp murder case, Sheriff Cannon and District Attorney Green claimed they were confidant that

Bradshaw was involved in her death, but their best witness, Luther Jolliff, had been freed on bond in November 1932 and had disappeared. On top of that, he had not seemed happy to testify against Bradshaw in the first place. Cannon had his doubts about his star witness. Authorities hoped they could find the uncooperative Jolliff and browbeat him into testifying. Jolliff had admitted bringing supplies to the killers, but denied his presence at the murder scene. If he was giving out names of suspects in the case, police were not telling the public at the time. Other potential witnesses in the Sharp case who had been contacted were playing deaf and blind in the matter. After watching witnesses in both cases come up missing under suspicious circumstances, who could blame them?

******

On July 29, Stillwell, Oklahoma, Chief of Police Chester Lee received a tip that "Skeet" Bradshaw and a pal, Bunks Patterson, were selling bootleg whiskey on a downtown street. Lee rounded up some fellow officers and went to investigate. When lawmen arrived at the scene where Bradshaw's car was parked, they called out to the pair to surrender. Patterson threw his hands up, but Bradshaw cursed the lawmen and fired a shot over their heads. Lee and his companions drew their weapons and returned fire. "Skeet" quickly gave up. The duo was arrested and "Skeet" was more than likely given a lesson on etiquette down at the station. They were both charged with whiskey violations when two gallons of "shiny" was found in the back seat of the car, along with several empty pint bottles and a funnel. Officers reported both men were roaring drunk. They obviously couldn't resist trying out their product. The following day Patterson pled guilty, inducing "Skeet" to do the same. Strangely, he was not charged with resisting arrest. "Skeet" was soon extradited to Chetopa, Kansas, where he sat in jail for a goodly long time, awaiting trial for robbing that town's bank.

******

Back in Muskogee County, brother Ford's lawyer demanded they try him or release him. Officials relented, granting the bandit a chance to make bond. They felt they needed more time to make their case, and with a large cash bond, they could retain some control over the "Vian Bad Boy." Bradshaw's father with the help of a Vian businessman came up with $4,000 cash to bond him out on August 5, 1933. In hindsight it was a very poor decision on the part of the Muskogee Court.

Chapter 6

A Bunch of Banks, and Webber Falls

In August 1933, Colonel Amos Woodcock, director of the National Prohibition Agency, reported that more arrests were made per capita in Oklahoma for alcohol violations than any other state. The state's Attorney General also issued a report, which stated the rate of bank robberies in the state had risen at a higher rate in the past three months than any other time in history. The only good news for lawmen in their efforts to get a handle on the ensuing crime wave was the capture in early August of one of the Kansas escapees, Harvey Bailey, in Paradise, Texas.

Capture of Harvey Bailey. Photo courtesy of Springfield News and Leader AP Photo.

After his release from jail, Bradshaw and his pals, Charlie Cotner and Ed Clanton, both of whom were wanted for a multitude of crimes, kept a low profile in August. Jim Benge was on the "scout" in parts unknown. Although there is some evidence that the gang went into the horse-theft and whiskey-hijacking business during this time, they stayed away from big hauls like banks for a spell.

****

Sometime in mid-August Wilber Underhill struck out on his own, leaving his fellow Kansas prison escapees to their own devises. During that period he traveled to Vian to see Hazel Hudson, his sweetheart, and his old prison buddy, Ford Bradshaw. Underhill was also an acquaintance of Charlie Cotner, who was a pal of Ed Davis, Wilber's companion in several robberies and another of the Kansas escapees. The outlaw and his girlfriend reportedly stayed at the Bradshaw place while in the grip of romance. The farm was long suspected by lawmen as being a cooling-off place for outlaws like Charlie Floyd and Bonnie and Clyde.

September 20, Bradshaw, Robert Trollinger, an uni-dentified man, and Charlie Dotson, an ex-con from Marble City who was married to a cousin of Kye Carlile, robbed the First National Bank of York, Nebraska, for $9,000. On the 22nd, Wilber Underhill and two unidentified confederates (one was believed to have been Charlie Cotner) robbed the Peoples National Bank in Stuttgart, Arkansas.

American National Bank, Baxter Springs, Kansas.

Underhill stood in the doorway with a machine gun while his two pals scooped up about a $1,000 from the tills. The fall of '33 turned out to be the most active period in the history of the gang.

At about noon on October 9, a 1933 maroon Chevy with license plate 483-183, carrying five men pulled up to the curb in front of the American National Bank of Baxter Springs, Kansas. One man suspected to have been Newt Clanton remained at the wheel of the car with the motor running while another man, thought to be either Robert Trollinger or Wilber Underhill, took up a position in front of the entrance to the bank. Bradshaw, Cotner and Clarence Eno, all dressed in fashionable powder blue suits and fedora hats, strode into the institution. Bradshaw ambled up to the window of cashier John Conrad and proclaimed, with a smile on his face, "I got 'ya covered, get 'em up." Cotner dashed behind the counter and began gathering up the cash out of the tills, putting the dough, about $3,000 in a pillowcase. Eno, with a sawed off shotgun, took a position in the center of the lobby, covering assistant cashier E. J. Whittaker, a janitor, and a customer. After ascertaining the vault was on a time lock, the three bandits took what plunder they could and left the bank, taking the two cashiers as hostages. After forcing their captives to ride on the car's running board for about a mile, Cotner told the bankers to hop off the moving car. Although authorities were quickly notified, the bandits were long gone before they could react. The chief of police and deputy were both out of town on the day of the robbery. The bandit's auto was last seen barreling down Route 66 at a high rate of speed. Many witnesses in town observed the robbery and they, including the bankers, all identified the robbers from mug shots as being the Cookson Hills bandits. The bank robbery in Baxter Springs was the first since 1914, when noted outlaw Henry Starr had stuck up the First National Bank there.

On the same day as the Baxter Springs robbery, Underhill and Ed Davis were positively identified by witnesses as the two villains who knocked off the Bank of Tryon, Oklahoma, for $550. Whether the pair was acting in concert with the Baxter Springs bandits is not known, but lawmen suspected as much. There is some controversy having to do with which robbery Underhill was actually involved. Although Underhill was identified by a witness, who had watched the robbery from across the street in Baxter Springs, Wilbur had actually introduced himself to the bank clerks in the Tryon, Oklahoma, robbery.

The following day in nearby Parsons, Kansas, "Skeet" Bradshaw's trial for the robbery of the Chetopa State Bank ended with the case going to the jury. During the trial a weeping Lulu Bradshaw, "Skeets" newly acquired wife and the niece of U. S. Congressman W. W. Hastings, swore on a stack of Bibles that on the very day and hour of the robbery, her then fiancé was on his knees asking for her hand in marriage. Bradshaw's father Jim also testified that his wayward son was in Stillwell on the day in question. Bradshaw's lawyer loudly proclaimed that his client could not have been in both places at the same time. A Chetopa merchant and a bank customer both testified that "Skeet" was one of the bandits in the raid. The jury returned after two hours with a verdict of not guilty. "Skeet" was released back to the bosom of his waiting family. One thing you had to say about the Bradshaws, they never went cheap on the hiring of top-notch legal talent.

****

On October 11, 1933, a few minutes past the noon hour, four unmasked men entered the International Bank of Haskell, Oklahoma, one carrying a machine gun. The man with the chopper issued a call of "Get 'em up." The cashier, W. E. Combs, and the teller, Dennis Rainwater, immediately complied. Jay Harris a black man who had been lounging on a bench in the bank, also threw his hands in the air. Two of the bandits walked behind the counter and began gathering the cash out of the tills. The pair rounded up about $1,000. The man with the machine gun remained in the center of the lobby while a fourth man stood at the main door armed with a sawed-off shotgun. The pair behind the counter, armed with pistols, demanded that the safe be opened. Combs responded that it was on a time clock set for 3 p.m. testily asking them if they had not seen the sign in the front window announcing that the safe was on a time lock. The lead bandit glared at him. At that point, Banker Rainwater said he nearly had a heart

The old International Bank building Haskell, Oklahoma, now a family clinic. Photo by Naomi Morgan.

attack and was dumbfounded that Combs had smarted off and was lecturing the gun-wielding robbers. The frustrated bandits made a little fuss, but knew it was useless and began herding the two bankers in front of them towards the getaway car. The outlaws piled in putting the bankers on the running boards and took off at a high rate of speed.

Several witnesses saw the robbery and one went to get the town constable. The officer lumbered down to the bank where a crowd had gathered. He questioned Jay Harris, who had been left behind by the bandits and was still holding his hands in the air. The constable called Sheriff Virgil Cannon in Muskogee who had his deputies set up roadblocks throughout the area. He also contacted the authorities in the surrounding counties, who also threw out a net of officers to try to snare the outlaws. Meanwhile, the thieves drove west a half-mile or so then went south to the main highway dumping their hostages off on the way. Several witnesses saw them speeding 70 or 80 miles per hour and heading towards Taft. The joke

Added defenses at Haskel Bank. The staircase leads to a little room above the vault where a guard would be on duty. There would be a little cut in the floor of the room above the vault. A person would be on watch with either a gun or a loaded canister of tear gas and sometimes they might be armed with both. This way they could be ready with a line a defense in case a robbery occurred. Insurance companies required this after a bank had been robbed. Photo by Naomi Morgan.

around Haskell for months afterwards was whether Banker Combs had asked the bandits for a receipt for the money taken. Old timers around Haskell still chuckle at the idea of the two bankers hanging on to the running boards, their fancy suit coats flapping in the wind. The robbery, the first ever in Haskell, caused quit a stir in the little town, giving people something to talk about on trade day besides the poor price of cotton. There were little tears or sadness over the event, since almost no one had money in the bank.

******

One person who probably did not appreciate the robbery of the bank in Haskell was Charles "Pretty Boy" Floyd, another bandit from the Cookson Hills. Floyd, by the time of the robbery, was one of the most wanted outlaws in America. He had few places to hide and one of those few was at his uncle-in-law Jess Ring's place, four miles south of Haskell. With the bank robbery, the Haskell area received an extraordinary amount of police attention. Actually, some area lawmen like Muskogee County Sheriff Virgil Cannon thought at first that Floyd was involved in the robbery. According to many elderly residents of the town, the bandit frequented the

Charles Floyd and Jess Ring, taken at the Jess Ring place near Haskell, Oklahoma. Photo courtesy of the Muskogee-Times.

town's social affairs, cafés and barbershops for several years, unscathed. The robbery and the attention it generated had put an end to that luxury.

Floyd, who was raised in Akins, about 13 miles east of the Bradshaw place, was according to numerous old-timers seen many times there. Rumor has it that earlier in Charlie and Ford Bradshaw's careers the pair conducted illegal whiskey business together. Several people who knew both men said Floyd often sat in on poker games played at the Bradshaw farm. One elderly gentleman tells the story of Floyd picking him up in front of the Bradshaw cabin in early 1934, giving him a ride to Vian. According to him, the bandit had a .45 automatic lying on the seat between them. The rider stated that when they arrived in town, Floyd gave him two dollars, telling him to "get a pint on me, and if anyone asks who you was riding with, just tell 'em a cousin."

****** ***

When the Haskell bankers and other witnesses looked at the mug books that afternoon, all agreed that Wilber Underhill, Ford Bradshaw, and Charlie Dotson were three of the robbers. Newt Clanton was suspected to have been the driver of the getaway car.

On October 17, Muskogee County Deputy Sheriff Marsh Cogan was informed by one of his sources that Charlie Dotson was in the Tahlequah area. He and Deputy Cash Russ immediately set off for the town where Cherokee County Deputy Grover Bishop joined them. They quickly surrounded Dotson at his hideout. After being informed of his impending demise by Bishop, who had no qualms about pulling a trigger on a man, Dotson thought better of resisting and gave up peacefully. He was transported to the Muskogee jail where the two Haskell Bank-

Charlie Dotson. Photo courtesy of the Muskogee-Phoenix.

ers identified him as one of the robbers. Dotson refused to implicate his accomplices no matter how much he was persuaded.

Within the week, the state of Nebraska demanded his extradition, due to his suspected participation in the York bank robbery there. A rumor was reported by the Muskogee newspapers, stating Wilber Underhill had sent word through the grapevine that if any lawmen tried to return Dotson to Nebraska, the officer would never make it back alive. Authorities must have taken the rumor seriously because Sheriff A. E. Carter of York, Nebraska, stated that when he came for his prisoner, if Oklahoma allowed extradition, a Federal marshal would accompany him.

******

Around this time, Marsh Corgan arrested Joe Harris, a twenty-four year old ex-con from Muskogee, on a charge of general suspicion, which they could do in those days. Harris, who possessed $900 in cash when he was arrested, had recently bought a new car and started sporting fancy suits and diamond-studded watches. Since he was a known thief who had been released from prison only six weeks previous and had no apparent legal means of support, Corgan had a feeling he was guilty of something. Soon after being arrested, he surprised lawmen by admitting that he was the driver in the York, Nebraska, bank job. His abrupt confession was a strange turn of events, since he was not even suspected in the crime. He gave his consent to be extradited back to Nebraska, where he promptly pled guilty and was sentenced to ten years in prison.

******

The next time the Cookson gang was heard from involved a wild night of revelry induced by too much corn whiskey. The affair cumulated in several vicious, inexcusable acts by the Bradshaws that can only be explained as pure meanness on their part.

In the late afternoon of October 22, the Bradshaw brothers, "Skeet" fresh out of jail from Chetopa, Kansas, where he had recently been acquitted of the crime of robbing the local bank, and Ford who had been fairly busy

Old jail for Webber Falls. Photo by Naomi Morgan.

himself up near Haskell, decided to raise some hell. Both men were reported as flaming drunk on local moonshine. They went on an evening drive, arriving in the little river town of Webber Falls where they were well known, being arrested for drunkenness and thrown in the town's small jail several times when they were in their teens. The duo drove up to a group of black men standing on a downtown street corner. "Skeet," obviously feeling his oats began verbally assaulting the group with racial epitaphs after one of the Negroes had the audacity to ask him for a match. The group did not take kindly to the vile words they were being called and said so, where upon "Skeet" pulled out a .38 caliber pistol and shot two of the men. The brothers then drove off chuckling to themselves as if they did not have a care in the world.

About two miles west of Webber Falls, Ford, who was driving, must have been distracted because he drove their car into a ditch, hitting a sizable oak tree. The pair then ambled into the middle of the road looking to catch a ride. James Cargile of Muskogee soon came tooling down the highway, minding his own business. When he saw two men in the road brandishing pistols, Cargile punched the accelerator, figuring there was no way he was stopping. The brothers unloaded their pistols into the speeding car, puncturing the radiator. Cargile paid no attention to the radiator, driving to a nearby farmhouse where he contacted the Sheriff's office in Muskogee.

Meanwhile back in town, comrades of the two wounded men found a local man who offered to drive the victims to the hospital in Muskogee. The two victims were loaded into the car, helped by the driver and another passenger, and headed to Muskogee for medical treatment. About two miles west of town, to their amazement they saw their two tormenters standing in the road pointing guns their way again. They pulled the car over to the side and raised their hands, but the brothers blasted the occupants with cruel indifference. Both men who had been wounded were hit again. The driver and passenger ran into the nearby woods unharmed. The Bradshaws threw the wounded out on the roadside and commandeered the car, driving it back to Webber Falls. On their arrival in town, the constable who had been investigating the earlier shootings sighted the brothers and opened fire on them with a deer rifle. The Bradshaws returned his fire, then fled town driving toward Warner.

Deputy Sheriffs Marsh Corgan and Bob Ledbetter, along with several other local law officers soon arrived in the area. After interviewing Mr. Cargile, the lawmen had a good idea who the pair of hijackers was. The Bradshaws were extremely well known to law enforcement officers in the area. The lawmen started driving toward Webber Falls in a three-car caravan. When they reached a point about one mile west of Webber Falls, a car came flying towards them at an excessive speed. The officers figured the occupants were the pair of drunken terrorists, and were half right. The Police caravan stopped while the speeding car passed them. The officers turned around and gave chase until the lead car carrying Deputy Corgan pulled up to the fleeing car and stuck a shotgun barrel in the driver's face. The driver pulled over and, sure enough, it carried "Skeet" Bradshaw, but no Ford was in sight. Bradshaw gave up peacefully, loudly claiming he had done no wrong. Officers found a jug of home brew on the floorboard along with a pistol. Bradshaw denied knowledge of either item. He also stated that he hadn't seen his brother for several days. The officers on the scene stated that the suspect was in a state of extreme drunkenness. It appears that brother Ford had gotten out of "Skeet's" car at the edge of town to visit with some fellow partygoers. He later stumbled into some nearby woods and passed out.

An ambulance was summoned to transport the wounded Negroes to Providence Hospital in Muskogee. The victims, Charles and George Green of rural Webber Falls, told officers they had not done a "damn thing" to incite the Bradshaws in their attack earlier in the evening. Both men were seriously wounded but would recover. "Skeet" was transported to the county jail where he was confined and charged with attempted murder.

Later that evening, Ford Bradshaw meandered out of the woods. Stationing himself in the middle of nearby Highway 64, he halted a car containing a schoolteacher, Bob Shinn of Webber Falls, who was driving with two young female passengers, Amy Walters and Fay Wadley. The victims later stated that Bradshaw threatened them with a pistol and hopped into the back seat of the car with one of the girls, ordering the driver to head to Beggs. On their arrival at the little town, he ordered the frightened driver to proceed to Henryetta, then Okemah, where he and his victims ate at a drive-in, threatening them with violence if they called attention to the vehicle. The car and its terrorized occupants were forced to accompany the outlaw, driving in circles the rest of the night. About 5 a.m. Bradshaw released the three a few miles outside of Okemah, giving each $5.00.

Meanwhile, dozens of area lawmen had begun searching the countryside for the slippery outlaw. A report was received of the kidnapping of Shinn and the girls. Their families spent a night in desperate worry over their well-being. Another report came in later that Sunday night of the four being sighted in Beggs. Officers rushed there, but came up empty handed. After the three were released, an APB was put out on the stolen car the suspect was driving. The car was found abandoned on a wooded road near Henryetta a week later.

It appears that after the Webber Falls incident, Charlie Cotner rounded up some of the gang members minus Bradshaw (who must of still been on a bender) and conducted another road trip. On October 24, the Merchants National Bank of Nebraska City, Nebraska was robbed of $6,135 by five heavily-armed men. The chief suspects were Charlie Cotner, Clarence and Otis Eno, Newt Clanton, and Robert Trollinger. Three employees were lined up against the walls while the gunmen looted the bank. The safe could not be entered due to a time lock. Two of the bankers, J. P. Gilligan and Elmo Shuey, were forced to ride on the running boards of the bandit's escaping vehicle for several blocks. The robbery was an exact replay of the October 9 Baxter Springs, Kansas job.

******

A few days later, at lunchtime, on October 30, a new dark colored Chevy sedan, pulled up next to the curb in

Galena National Bank, Galena, Kansas. Photo by Naomi Morgan.

front of the Galena National Bank Galena, Kansas. Three men disgorged from the vehicle, entering the institution. Two cashiers, A. H. Moorman and T. C. Moeller, along with one customer were in the bank at the time. One of the men, later identified as Charlie Cotner, strode up to Moeller thrusting a sawed off shotgun in his face and ordered him to "stay still and shut up." Another man, Ford Bradshaw, leaped over the counter with a sack in hand and started harvesting the cash from the tills. A third man, Clarence Eno, stood in the lobby armed with a sub machinegun. A few minutes into the robbery M. A. Parker, a seventy-year old gray-headed lady, walked into the bank. She was made to sit on the floor. After gathering up about $3,000, the trio calmly ordered the two bankers to accompany them to their waiting car, and were instructed by Bradshaw to "mount up boys." The frightened cashiers were let off a few blocks out of town. One of the cashiers later described the back seat of the bandit's vehicle as loaded down with shotguns and rifles of every sort.

The alarm was spread quickly throughout the community. Two Galena officers and a fireman jumped in their car and attempted to cut off the bandits by using a short-cut. They sighted the bandit's speeding car about a mile south of town. A brief gunfight ensued but the officers quickly backed off. Near Fairland, Oklahoma, Ottawa County Sheriff Waters, and a deputy also sighted the outlaws. Another short but furious gun battle erupted between the two parties. When the lawmen's car was hit in the fender and radiator, they also pulled out of the chase. There was nothing more seen of the fleeing gunmen. The employees and witnesses from the bank later confirmed the identities of the robbers. A man named Crocket told police that the trio got gas at his station a few minutes before the heist. After this robbery, the gang temporarily split up. Eno left

Bradshaw and Cotner off at Chelsea where they met up with Eddy Clanton. The following day, Clanton's brother drove the trio back to the Cooksons. The same day the Kansas Bankers Association announced a reward of $250 would be paid for the capture of bank robbers, dead or alive.

On November 2, around the noon hour, four well-dressed men entered the Citizens National Bank of Okmulgee. The bank's vice president, J. H. McElroy, later stated to police that the men entered the bank off the Sixth Street entrance. One of the bandits ordered the employees to stand back from their workstations and be still. All the men were armed with pistols except one man standing in the doorway who was armed with a sawed-off shotgun. A tall sandy haired man identified as Ford Bradshaw announced, "This is a holdup." McElroy, who thought someone was playing a practical joke, laughed at the man. One of the bandits later identified as Wilber Underhill who possessed absolutely no sense of humor, snarled, "This is not a joking matter." The seven employees and two customers in the bank immediately complied with the bandit's instructions.

The Citizens National Bank of Okmulgee circa 1930s. Photo courtesy of the Okmulgee Public Library.

All the tills and safes but one that was on a time lock were rifled. Two customers entered the bank unexpectedly and were prodded to join the rest of the group by the man holding a shotgun, sawed off to the size of a large pistol, at the door. A few minutes later an Indian woman entered the bank and was told to "come in and sit on the floor," a statement she didn't understand since she spoke little English. The bandit at the door, suspected to have been Charlie Cotner, repeated his order to her, but ran out of patience when the woman attempted to leave the bank. He grabbed her by the hair and wrestled her to the floor. Underhill ordered bank teller O. H. Kirk to open the vault that was time locked, threatening to blow his head off if he didn't comply. Witnesses state that a smaller bandit, identified as Newt Clanton, came forward and cooled off the taller bandit, telling him to "forget it." Underhill also asked if McElroy would say hello to John Russell for him. Russell had been the Sheriff of Okmulgee County in the 1920s, who once transported Underhill to prison. McElroy and Kirk were made to walk in front of the bandits to their car

Inside of the Citizens National Bank of Okmulgee circa 1930s. Photo courtesy of the Okmulgee Public Library.

out front as they fled the bank. The bankers were then told to "hop up on the running boards and hang on." The driver of the getaway car, Clarence Eno, backed out towards the street, struck a parked car, then accelerated east. At the corner of Central Avenue and Fifth Street near a lumberyard, the two bankers were kicked off the running boards of the moving car. The two victims watched the vehicle flee in an easterly direction, then ran to the lumberyard to call the police. Neither of the bankers was injured except for a few bumps and bruises due to being pushed off the car.

Sheriff John Lennox sent his deputies to several sights around the county to set up roadblocks, but to no avail. After interviewing the witnesses at the bank and having them survey his mug books, there was no doubt who the perpetrators were. When banker McElroy formally identified Underhill as one of the bandits, he described him as an "unattractive, rangy looking fellow, dark haired with a snaggletooth." An all-points bulletin was sent out throughout the Midwest for the bandits and their car.

Main Street of Okmulgee circa 1920s. Photo courtesy of the Okmulgee Public Library.

The gateway car, a black 1933 Chevy, was found the next day two miles southeast of Henryetta. Luther Houk, who lived nearby, reported he had witnessed an automobile arrive at the spot, and minutes later another car drove up. He stated:

"The occupants of the first car disgorged, and were soon joined by the men riding in the second car. They stood around drinking whiskey from a pint bottle for a few minites, then they all hopped into the second car and drove away."

The owner of the abandoned car was identified as Elizabeth Barnes, an Okmulgee schoolteacher, who along with a friend, Mary Hasey, had been forced off the road by two armed men on October 10, a mile north of Beggs. The pair of hijackers who they later identified as Wilber Underhill and Eddie Clanton kidnapped the women for several hours. The ladies stated Underhill had proposed to Clanton that they kill the pair, but Clanton nixed the idea, talking Underhill into releasing the women. Authorities reported the schoolteacher's car had 800 miles on the odometer when stolen and over 8,000 miles on it when recovered. The take from the Okmulgee robbery was about $14,000, a hell of a chunk of money in 1933.

Chapter 7

Vian, Okmulgee, Big Jim and Nebraska

On Saturday November 5, 1933, about eight that evening Constable Walter Thornton of Vian, Oklahoma, was checking the doors of local businesses making sure they were secure. He looked up and saw three carloads of people driving up behind him. Suddenly someone shouted, "Shoot him." Thornton, seized with panic, craned his neck and saw two well-known characters in the front seat of the lead car, Ford Bradshaw and Charlie Cotner. He also recognized the figure of Wilber Underhill, who was in the backseat, from wanted posters. He knew that all three men

Inside of Vian Drug Store and Vian townspeople circa 1932. Photo courtesy of Herbert Dennis of Vian

were violent criminals, wanted for numerous robberies and murders. Thornton, in an act of desperation, ran to a corner building that he had a key to and let himself in. The cars, loaded down with outlaws, drove by shooting out a window in the establishment and hurling threats his way. The constable picked up the phone and called his fellow Vian peace officers, Curtus Hammond and Wes Hammett. Both officers arrived at the building where Thornton was holed up within minutes.

The caravan of bad men cruised the main drag for an hour shooting out a window here and there, and shouting out threats against the lawmen, who had decided to stay in the locked building for the time being. The three officers, armed with only pistols, were no match for the gang of

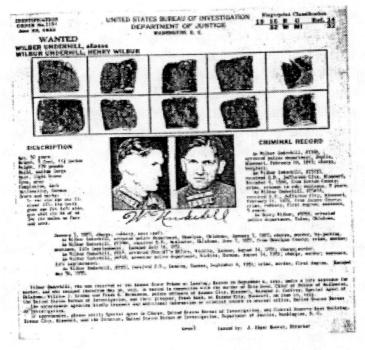

Wilber Underhill's wanted poster. Courtesy of Mike Koch.

thugs, who allegedly kept a machine gun trained on the building they had sought refuge in. They called for reinforcements from Sallisaw and Muskogee.

The trouble appeared to have started when Officer Thornton received word from the grapevine earlier that afternoon that Bradshaw and company was going to kill him. The outlaw claimed that the local police had been harassing female members of his family and questioning them in a rough manner. Several women were sighted in the caravan cruising the Vian streets that evening. Earlier that night a local farmer named Walters who lived a short distance from the Bradshaw place had his windows shot out by the same procession of cars. Authorities never figured out what connection, if any Walters had with the outlaws.

Meanwhile, six carloads of officers came streaming out of Muskogee to assist their comrades. When Sheriff Cannon's minions, numbering about fifteen officers and special deputies that made up the entire Sheriff department, arrived there was no sign of the suspects, who had melted back into the nearby Cooksons. Other officers numbering about twenty soon arrived from McIntosh County and nearby Sallisaw. A manhunt into the heavily timbered hills ensued. That night and into the next day lawmen combed the area north and east of Vian, questioning locals, who were of little assistance. The code of the hills in those days was to mind your own business, and never associate with outsiders, especially lawmen. About 8 p.m. the next evening, Underhill, Bradshaw, Cotner, and others reportedly ambushed a small group of officers in a heavily forested region which was pocketed with caves, near Marble City. The posse retreated in chaos towards Sallisaw. No one was hurt, but it was a great humiliation for the police officers involved.

******

The other gang members were heard from next when a group of officers raided an apartment in Bristow, Oklahoma, on November 10. Police arrested Clarence Eno, a suspect in the Okmulgee Bank robbery, along with his brother Otis, who was Bradshaw's brother-in-law. Otis, suffering from a gunshot wound in the foot, was passed out on the couch in a stupor when the raid occurred. He had apparently shot himself accidentally while cleaning his rifle. Arresting the Eno bothers probably didn't bother them a wit as they were seasoned pros. Clarence had done time in Oklahoma in 1926-29 for auto theft, then drew five more years in Kansas in '29 for burglary. He was released in 1930 and immediately jumped parole. He was again arrested and convicted in Oklahoma for attempted murder. After serving two years in McAlester he was transferred to Kansas to do a term for parole violation. He escaped in October 1932. Brother Otis's life followed the same pattern as his brother. He was convicted of the same auto theft charge as his brother in 1926, and then escaped prison. He was recaptured in 1930 and sent to the Oklahoma State Penitentiary where he was paroled in August 1932. Otis was another of Ford Bradshaw's prison pals and shortly after his release from the pen he joined up with the Cookson Hills bunch. Brother Clarence also joined the outfit soon after he was sprung from the big house.

Also apprehended in the raid were Eno's mother and Hazel Wind. Creek County authorities charged Ms. Wind for harboring the bandits. Mary Eno, the boys' mother was soon released. According to the officers, Wind was also suspected of harboring Ford Bradshaw, off and on, over a several-month period. Bradshaw was not present in the apartment, but informants said he had been there many times. She had previously spent time in jail for harboring another bandit, John Tudor, who was captured in the same Bristow apartment the year before and convicted of robbing the Bank of Sedan, Kansas. He was sentenced to twenty years in the Kansas State Prison. Wind was released on bond from the Creek County Jail in Sapulpa a few weeks later. About a $1,000 in small bills was found in the apartment, which was thought to be part of the proceeds from the Okmulgee robbery. The day following the raid authorities, who had been keeping the Bristow apartment under surveillance, spotted Bradshaw's sister Rema Deetjen, her husband, and Gypsy Bradshaw Eno trying to enter the dwelling. Police arrested the group who claimed they had just come calling on the Eno's for a social visit. They all swore they knew nothing of the Eno brothers' nefarious activities. The trio were held in the Creek county jail for several days then released.

On November 12, Okmulgee banker J. H. McElroy was brought to Creek County to view the Eno brothers and positively identified Clarence Eno as one of the robbers. The brothers were transferred to the Okmulgee County jail the next day, where it was thought they would be tried for the Okmulgee Bank job. Otis made bond several days after his arrest, but Clarence was refused bail, because he was judged a habitual offender, and a flight risk.

******

The following day a man came stumbling into a business in Braggs, claiming he had been kidnapped and his car stolen the night before. When Muskogee County deputies questioned the man he gave his name as A. W. Welch. He said that at 9 p.m. the previous evening he was getting into his car in front of the Boulevard Christian Church in

Muskogee when two armed men approached him, forcing him into his parked car and driving towards Braggs Mountain. At the top of the hill, they turned onto a side road and met up with a carload of men. He stated he was booted out of his car onto the road and given $2.00 by the hijackers before they drove off, leaving him several miles away from civilization. He identified Ford Bradshaw and Wilber Underhill as his kidnappers.

The same day, Nebraska authorities with the assistance of three Federal marshals picked up and transported Charlie Dotson to Nebraska for trial in the York bank robbery where several witnesses had identified him as one of the bandits. Oklahoma authorities held a retainer on Dotson for the robbery of the Haskell Bank. The agreement between the two states was if Dotson were found innocent of the charges in Nebraska, he would be transported back to Oklahoma to be tried for the Haskell job. Dotson's luck ran out on December 8, when he was found guilty and sentenced to twenty-five years at hard labor. He was received at the Nebraska State Penitentiary at Lincoln the following day as inmate #11790.

******

On November 15 it was announced in the Muskogee Court that Ford Bradshaw's bond had been revoked and the money put towards the bond would be seized. Muskogee County court officers stated that without the influx of cash from the seizure the court would have been without funds and would have had to put off the current court session until a later date. Bradshaw's father, who had put up most the cash, nearly $4,000, fought the decision but to no avail. The District Attorney also announced that "Skeet" Bradshaw, who was currently being held in the County jail on two charges of attempted murder, would also be charged with a federal whiskey violation stemming from the incident in Stillwell.

Eighty miles away in Coalgate, Oklahoma, a bold Wilber Underhill strolled into the Coal County courthouse on November 18 with his sweetheart, Hazel Hudson, asking for a marriage licence. The license he received was made out to the woman and Henry W. Underhill, Wilber's real name. The happy couple then strolled down to a barbershop run by the Reverend C. A. Magness who performed the nuptials for the lovebirds. Not being the romantic type, Wilber dumped the little woman back at their hideout near Vian and celebrated his honeymoon by traveling to Frankfort, Kentucky, where he and several others robbed a local bank. It was not known who his associates were.

******

On November 25, Clarence Eno and four other inmates overpowered the night jailer at the Okmulgee County Jail and fled into the night. The escapees were identified as Eno, Otis Shular, Earl Williams, Larry Wiesnor, and James Quinn. Evidently, Williams, a jail trustee, had gotten hold of an ice pick from the jail's kitchen and held it to the jailer's throat until he handed him the keys. He then locked the poor man in an empty cell and unlocked several cells belonging to the four other prisoners. The group then proceeded to unlock and raid the jails armory, collecting a shotgun and several pistols. The jailor, Donald Loomis, begged the inmates confined in the bullpen area to call out for assistance, since their barred windows faced the street. The prisoners laughed at Loomis' predicament.

Meanwhile, the five escapees came upon a car parked

next to the Log Cabin Café, located near the jail. The two persons setting in the auto were rudely ejected and the inmates drove off with a squall of rubber, however, not before an off-duty cop and several bystanders saw them. The Okmulgee city police officer and two cars loaded with vigilantes followed the escapees several miles into the country, when suddenly the escapee's car stopped and the inmates fled into a patch of nearby woods. The posse soon lost them in the Deep Fork river bottoms. Back in Okmulgee, the embarrassed jailor was released and the National Guard was called in. The Guardsmen formed an armed perimeter around the jail to prevent any further escape attempts.

******

On November 27, Sheriff Cannon received a tip that Jim Benge, who hadn't been heard from since February when he allegedly participated in holding up several cars at the bandit's roadblock near Webber Falls, was living with his wife in a shack nine miles south of Bartlesville. The Sheriff, accompanied by his deputies, Marsh Corgan and Bob Ledbetter, along with several local lawmen surrounded the cabin. Cannon pounded on the door demanding Benge's surrender. A dog came snarling out of the front door and was immediately shot. Soon afterwards Benge came bursting out the back door where officers confronted him with shotguns. Corgan told the handsome bandit, "You move another step you'll die." Benge must have believed him because he quickly raised his hands telling the lawmen that he "knew when he was licked." The prisoner was transported back to the Muskogee County jail where a charge of murdering Susie Sharp as well as a host of other charges awaited him. He also faced a charge of armed robbery in Okmulgee County where he had been identified as one of the bandits who participated in the November 7, 1932, robbery of the American Exchange Bank in Henryetta with Ford Bradshaw and "Newt" Clanton. The alleged killer plead not guilty at his preliminary the following morning. After the capture of Benge, Cannon stated in an interview that the push was on to catch the remaining suspects in the Sharp killing. Asked if officers had any leads on the whereabouts of Bradshaw or Clanton, Cannon said he predicted that the pair as well as the missing Luther Jolliff would be in custody in short order.

******

In early December, Underhill and his crew arrived back in the eastern Oklahoma area. On December 12, the bandit tried to steal a safe from the First National Bank of Harrah. While the gang was dragging it to the car: the heavy safe fell through the floor of the bank into the basement. After this unexpected development, the thieves gave up on the project and fled the area with empty pockets. The burglars had plenty of time to conduct their business, since they had kidnapped the town constable at gunpoint. The bandits later released him unharmed.

On December 13, Underhill and two companions,

Elmer Inman. Photo courtesy of Kansas Department of Corrections.

probably Ralph Roe and Elmer Inman, dressed up in fancy suits, hopped in Wilber's new car, and headed to Coalgate, Oklahoma. The men entered the First National Bank at about 11 a.m. leveling a machine gun at cashiers Oliver Browning and

Frank Collete. Underhill, doing the talking, told the freighted cashiers "This is a robbery and you have some money I want." Wilber was never known for his tact.

Cashier Browning was ordered to open the safe. When he replied that it was on a timer, Underhill insisted he try. When the banker tried the safe's door, it opened. Browning expressed shock, but Wilber was not amused. About $3,000 was gathered up in cash and coin. Browning and a fellow cashier along with three bank customers were forced to accompany the bandits to their getaway car. The five were made to hop on the running boards to act as human shields. The hostages were given their freedom on the outskirts of town with a gentle nudge from Underhill off the moving car. The fleeing auto was last seen heading towards Ada at a high rate of speed.

The next morning, a Konawa police officer reported to Seminole Police Chief Jake Sims that he had witnessed a car that matched the description of the bandit's vehicle

Early Seminole, Oklahoma, Police Force circa late 1920s. Photo courtesy of the Seminole County Historical Society.

turn off Highway 39 into the hills late the night before. That afternoon Sims and a posse drove five miles south of Konawa to the home of George Nash, who was the father of Houston Nash, a known associate of Underhill. The elder Nash was suspected of harboring fugitives in the past. Sims walked to the front door of the house where he started talking to the elder Nash while the posse took up stations, mainly towards the rear of the residence. Suddenly Underhill, clothed only in his underwear, jumped out a side window of the home and raced to his new car sitting in the driveway. Before Sims or his posse could react, the outlaw was long gone. The embarrassed lawmen had to be satisfied with waiting around for the younger Nash to arrive home which he did, with Bruce Brady, brother of Bob who had escaped in May with Wilber from the Kansas State Prison. Brady was held for Federal authorities who had a warrant for his arrest, and Houston Nash was detained on suspicion of participating in the Coalgate robbery. A machine gun and several pistols along with a bag of coins were found in the house.

****

Around the same time, Jim Benge's preliminary was held at the Muskogee County courthouse. The handsome bandit's lawyer loudly proclaimed, that his client was innocent of the charges leveled against him. The Judge did not concur, and bound him over for trial. The defendant was also refused a chance at making bond. His honor mused that if he granted the outlaw bail, he'd "get rabbit" and go back on the scout. Later that day, the same Judge, J. F. Beavers, also refused "Skeet" Bradshaw the opportunity to go free on bond, citing he was a flight risk.

News of Ford Bradshaw's group was noted on December 22, 1933, when Syracuse, Nebraska, authorities reported the robbery of the First National Bank by three gunmen. Six witnesses at the bank positively identified two of the three bandits through mug shots as Ford Bradshaw and Clarence Eno, who had recently escaped from the Okmulgee County Jail. Syracuse, a small farming community of about 900 people, sits about eight miles from Nebraska City in the southeast corner of the state, the scene of the gang's October 1933 robbery. Otoe County Sheriff Carl Ryder stated that shortly before noon three armed men entered the bank, robbing it of $1,500. The bankers and customers were lined up against a wall while the bandits looted the bank. Two bank employees, Charles Andrews and W. C. Lamberth, were abducted and released on the outskirts of town. After an intense two-state manhunt, there was no sign of the robbers.

Later that month on December 30 Bradshaw, Cotner, Bullet Roland, Mount Cookson, and seventy year old "Kaiser" Bill Goodman robbed the National Bank of Mansfield, Arkansas of $1,700. Officers converged on the town, but the bandits, taking the back roads, fled into the nearby vastness of the Cooksons. Rumor has it, there was a violent quarrel between gang members over the stolen proceeds after this robbery. Evidently, one of the bandits tried to pocket some of the stolen money before it was dumped in the kitty to be evenly divided. So much for honor among thieves. Incedentally, years later an elderly gentleman admitted that Bradshaw had asked him to participate in the heist as a lookout. The old man, a reliable fellow, stated that he didn't take him up on the offer, but was sorly tempted, as hard as times were.

Chapter 8

A Mad Dog Bites the Dust, Enos, and Bradshaws

R. H. Colvin, head of the US Department of Justice in Oklahoma City, got involved in the case on June 17, 1933, when a fellow Justice Department officer was killed escorting the notorious Frank "Jelly" Nash from Hot Springs, Arkansas, to Kansas City, Missouri. When a train carrying the officers arrived at Kansas City's Union Station, the lawmen along with their prisoner walked to the parking lot where several hidden assailants fired upon the group from several directions. US Department of Justice Agent Ray Caffrey, two Kansas City police officers, an Oklahoma officer, and prisoner Frank Nash were killed in the barrage. Department of Justice Director J. Edger Hoover put a top priority on catching the killers. Among the individuals that authorities first suspected in the assault were Charlie Floyd, Adam Richetti, Verne Miller, and all

Frank Nash. Courtesy Okmulgee Daily Times.

the1933 Memorial Day escapees from the Kansas State Prison. Since Wilber Underhill was among the latter group and known to have been at liberty at the time of the killings, he became a prime suspect. Hoover notified his entire department to put a priority on Underhill's capture, although the likelihood of Underhill being involved seemed slim.

Colvin was not able to make any progress on the case until five months later when an informant told him of a beauty shop in Shawnee, Oklahoma, which the killer was suspected of using for a meeting place. After a few days of watching the business, Colvin's agents spotted Ralph Roe, an Underhill associate whose girlfriend, Eva Nichols, worked in the shop. Lawmen followed the pair to a frame home at 606 West Dewey Street in Shawnee. Agent Colvin gathered re-enforcements, which included four other Federal agents, three Oklahoma City officers, several Oklahoma County deputies, and a Shawnee police captain.

At 3 a.m. December 30, 1933, the same day the Bradshaw bunch knocked over the Mansfield, Arkansas,

Scene at the Union Station massacre. Photo courtesy of the Springfield News and Leader –AP Photo

bank, the posse surrounded the bungalow. When officers called out to Underhill to surrender, he responded by firing out a window at the lawmen. The posse answered with a volley of machine gun and shotgun fire. Suddenly, Wilber came flying out the front door in his long-handle underwear at a dead run. Officers blasted the outlaw numerous times with shotguns and rifles. Underhill dropped to the ground several times, but kept scurrying until he made it to the shadows between two houses. Officers searched the surrounding area with no success. A massive citywide search that was impeded by a dense fog that had set in was conducted with the help of bloodhounds, but to no avail. When officers entered the cottage, they found a slightly wounded Ralph Roe and his badly injured girlfriend, Eva Nichols. Underhill's new bride was found under a bed miraculously uninjured. All were placed in police custody or in the city hospital under heavy guard. For the rest of that day and into the evening dozens of curiosity seekers tromped through the crime scene-stealing souvenirs. The homeowner publicly demanded that the police retrieve several pieces of property which had been stolen from the furnished rental house.

A call came into the police station at dawn about a man in his underwear breaking into a downtown furniture store over a mile from the shootout site. On arriving at the business, officers found a badly bleeding Underhill collapsed and barely alive in a heap on the floor. He had thirteen bullets in his body. Underhill was taken to the Shawnee City Hospital where doctors announced that he was near death. A heavy cordren of police were placed at the hospital. When grilled by the FBI over the next few days, an often-delirious Underhill confessed to numerous bank robberies, some of which he was involved, some of which he was not. The killer refused to take credit for several crimes that authorities were certain he had committed.

Miss Nichols died the next day and was buried at Maple Grove Cemetery in Seminole. Roe survived and was sent to the Oklahoma State Prison, and later transferred to Alcatraz Federal Prison. Underhill amazingly survived another week but died on January 6, 1934, after being transferred to the pen at McAlester on the orders of J. Edger Hoover. The motivation for moving the

Wilber Underhill. Photo courtesy of the Okmulgee Public Library

badly wounded Underhill was the Director's reaction to rumors that the Cookson Hills Gang and others were planning to rescue him from the clutches of the law. Several days later, when Underhill was buried in Joplin, Missouri, over 2,000 curiosity seekers showed up at the Ozark Memorial Park Cemetery to gawk at the bandit's mortal remains. Underhill, who had been dubbed the "Tri-State Terror" by the newspapers, had been one of the most violent and active of the Public Enemies of the '30s. His demise was a relief to lawmen throughout the Midwest.

The day after Underhill was captured, Bradshaw, with Cotner, Clanton, and several others, got liquored up after hearing the news and went on a tear. Again, the victim of their wrath was the little town of Vian. Citizens witnessed the gang shoot windows out of the Huggins hardware store, a restaurant, and the city jail. They whooped and hollered and terrorized the town half the night. For some odd reason there was no officer on duty, and by the time lawmen arrived from Sallisaw and Muskogee the outlaws were long gone.

According to County Attorney J. Fred Green, the gang was either angry over Underhill's arrest or just got drunk and felt mean that New Years Eve. In the early morning hours of the next day, witnesses observed Ford Bradshaw visiting Muskogee's Vendome Hotel, located due north of the present day Connors State College building. Bradshaw was evidently looking for a woman who lived in the hotel. The doorman wouldn't allow the drunken bandit into the building, so Bradshaw beat the poor man half to death with his gun butt and fled the scene. The doorman survived, but was left permanently disfigured.

Later that morning, New Years Day, Bradshaw, Cotner, and Clanton abandoned a car in Tahlequah and stole another off the city streets belonging to a local attorney named Joe Stone. The trio pulled into a local gas station on the outskirts of town. While filling the freshly stolen car with fuel, attendant Joe Brown noticed a machine gun in the back seat. Alarmed, he called Deputy Sheriff Grover Bishop after the group had left. Bishop, who was a formidable force in his own right, set up a roadblock near the Braggs cutoff. The bandits drove right past him a few minutes later. The deputy was unlucky that day, his car got stuck in the mud just minutes after he and another deputy started their pursuit.

Ralph Roe. Photo courtesy of the Muskogee-Times

Bishop only managed to shoot the fleeing car's back window, shattering it as they raced by his position.

During the evening of January 8, Bradshaw's 59-year-old father was driving down the wrong side of the road north of his home when he was hit head on by a bus from the Southern Kansas Stage Lines. Louis Brockman from Vian, riding in the passenger seat, stated he had warned Bradshaw seconds before the accident to be careful and stay on his side of the road. The impact killed Bradshaw instantly, Brockman suffered only slight injuries. The car was totaled. When informed of his father's death, "Skeet" Bradshaw, who was residing in the Muskogee County jail, burst into tears. The elder Bradshaw was his strongest supporter, getting him a lawyer and trying to establish a bond for his release. Jim Bradshaw was buried at the small family graveyard a couple hundred yards down a valley near the Bradshaw cabin. The crowd at his funeral was estimated to be over 500 citizens. Also attending was a manacled "Skeet" Bradshaw, whom Sheriff Virgil Can-

The streets of Vian today. Photo by Naomi Morgan.

non had allowed to attend in the company of several deputies.

Earlier that day, officers determined that the nearly new Chevrolet, which Jim Bradshaw was driving at the time of the accident, had been registered to Blanche Cotner, sister of outlaw Charlie Cotner. The same woman had also purchased the auto Underhill was in possession of at the time of his capture. A suit which had been brought against the bus line by the Bradshaw family was dismissed the following week. The judge determined that the accident was not the fault of the bus driver, but due to negligence on the part of the elder Bradshaw.

On the day of the funeral, several US Department of Justice agents, and county officers who had been hot on Ford Bradshaw's trail, were busy trying to set up an ambush for the outlaw hoping that he would try to attend his Father's funeral to pay his last respects. Actually, Bradshaw's relatives and in-laws still tell the story of Ford helping his mother pick out his father's coffin. While he was at it he also picked out his own. He must have sensed his own end was near. His daddy's casket, an expensive bronze type, was set up in the parlor of the Bradshaw cabin the night before the funeral. Agents watching the cabin saw no sign of the bandit. But Federal Agent Dan Dever and Deputy Marsh Corgan, manning a checkpoint north of the farm on Highway 17, observed a speeding car rush past their position. The lawmen reacted quickly, pursuing the fast moving vehicle. When the officers caught up with the car they recognized Ford Bradshaw in the passenger seat and Charlie Cotner driving. Bradshaw poked a rifle barrel out the window and cut loose with a couple of rounds at the lawmen. The fleeing car slowed and made a sudden turn down a dirt road, which was a cutoff leading to Fort Smith. The pursuing officers quickly got lost on the winding, hilly roads, and decided to drive back to Sallisaw and call Fort Smith authorities.

Fort Smith officers rapidly set up a roadblock near the foot of the Arkansas River bridge leading into the city. Sure enough, the bandits' speeding car came barreling towards them about five minutes after they established their position. Bradshaw cut loose with his rifle and Cotner was reported firing a pistol. The officers manning the roadblock dived under their cars and into the ditch along the roadway. The outlaw's new Chevy banged into the officers' car in the road but sped on across the bridge. The policemen last saw the car ripping down Garrison Avenue heading downtown where it was lost from sight.

******

Bottom L-R: Lula Bradshaw, (wife of Skeet) unknown, and Gypsy Bradshaw Eno. Top L-R: Tom Abel and Skeet Bradshaw. Photo courtesy of the Vian Press

On January 19, 1934, Wilber Underhill's fellow Memorial Day escapees, Bob Brady and Jim Clark who had been captured in October of '33 in New Mexico and transferred back to the Kansas State Prison, made another bid for freedom. The pair, along with five other inmates, overpowered a guard and went over the wall. They stole a schoolteacher's car and fled towards Oklahoma. Near Paola, Kansas, the escapees were spotted crossing a farmer's field. The local

Sheriff was called and he and a small posse approached the men. A gunfight ensued in which Brady was killed. Clark was captured a few months later after he participated in a minor crime spree. He was sent to Federal prison where he served thirty-five years before being paroled in 1969. He died in Oklahoma in 1971.

******

On January 25, four members of the Bradshaw gang staged a raid on the bank at Wellington, Kansas, stealing $4,000. Clarence and Otis Eno along with Ford Bradshaw were positively identified as three of the four bandits involved in the affair. Charles White of Sallisaw was later identified as the fourth man. On January 29, a Tulsa City police officer spotted Bradshaw entering an apartment on the city's north side which was rented to a woman named Williams. Preparations were made for a dawn raid on the residence. At 5 a.m. a horde of Oklahoma and Kansas lawmen led by Tulsa Detective Mark Lairmore, armed with machine guns and tear gas bombs, smashed in the doors

Tulsa detectives circa 1930s. Photo courtesy of John Lairmore son of Detective Mark Lairmore

and windows, forcibly entering the apartment. The lawmen again captured the Eno brothers, Clarence and Otis, but Bradshaw somehow slipped away unseen.

Also arrested in the raid were three women, later identified as Ford Bradshaw's sister Clara "Gypsy" Eno, wife of Otis, Dorothy Campbell, and once again Mary Eno, mother of the bandit brothers. The elderly Eno woman had in her possession $1,900 in small bills. It was later established that the old lady was not only the mother of the two presently captured bandits, but had three other sons, all doing time in various prisons. Gypsy Eno also had in her possession $870 in mostly five and ten dollar bills. A variety of handguns, including two Lugars with shoulder stocks that were fully automatic weapons, several shotguns and rifles, were a found on the premises.

Several days after the raid, old lady Eno was released with the money when the insurance companies could not identify it as belonging to any of several banks. Gypsy Eno and Dorothy Campbell were kept in jail and charged with harboring fugitives from justice. Among the numerous charges against Otis Eno was one of bigamy. A Cushing, Oklahoma, woman had come forward to file this charge against him when she found out that Otis had married the Bradshaw woman without the benefit of getting a divorce from her.

The two brothers were extradited back to Kansas to face numerous charges of armed robbery and conspiracy to kidnap Peggy Landon, the daughter of Kansas Governor Alf Landon. The kidnapping charge was based on information provided by an informant who claimed Clarence Eno along with his brother Otis, Charlie Cotner, and Glenn Leroy Wright were planning to snatch the Governor's pride and joy to force him to grant executive clemency to six of their associates being held in the Kansas prison system.

The plan was never carried out and the charges were later dropped for lack of evidence. On February 23, Clarence and Otis Eno were found guilty of the armed robbery of the Wellington Bank, and were sentenced to twenty to one hundred years in the Kansas State Prison.

******

Back in Tahlequah, Oklahoma, Charles Dotson's blond wife was charged with assisting in the robbery of the Midland, Arkansas Bank along with "Kaiser" Bill Goodman and Mount Cookson. When the bankers came forward to identify her, they reneged saying the woman they saw at the time of the robbery was blond like Mrs.

Mrs. Charles Dotson. Photo courtesy of the Muskogee-Phoenix

Dotson, but was covered with freckles. Dotson had not a freckle one. The bank robbery charge was dropped, but she wasn't out of the woods yet. The FBI arrested her on the courthouse steps after her hearing. She was charged with auto theft across state lines, a federal charge. It seems that Mrs. Dotson had been driving, at the time of her arrest, a car stolen in Arkansas and identified as being used in several crimes committed by the Cookson Hills gang.

Chapter 9

Bullets Flying, and the Big Raid

In the early evening hours of February 3, Creek County Sheriff Willis Strange received a phone tip informing him of the presence of several suspicious characters hiding out in small two-room shack on the outskirts of Sapulpa, Oklahoma. The residence, located off Route 66 near the old Liberty Glass Company belonged to Lee Davis, an elderly truck farmer. The call was the beginning of a bloody and violent weekend that would be long remembered by citizens and lawmen in Oklahoma.

Chief Tom Brumley killed at the Sapulpa shootout. Photo courtesy of the Sapulpa Herald.

The Sheriff, who suspected the persons in question might be the individuals responsible for a recent spat of area filling station robberies, gathered a posse and rushed to the scene. Soon after officers surrounded the residence, a fierce gunfight broke out between officers and several outlaws hiding inside. Two lawmen, Sapulpa Chief of Police Tom Brumley and Patrolman C. F. Lloyd were killed in the clash. Also killed was twenty-two year old Aussie (real name Aulcie)

Police Office C. F. Lloyd killed at the Sapulpa shootout. Photo courtesy of the Sapulpa Herald.

Elliott, a violent hoodlum with a long criminal record who had once been a member of "Pretty Boy" Floyd's gang, and a jewel thief named Delbert Carolan of Stigler, Oklahoma. A third suspect, Eldon Wilson of Tulsa, Elliott's long-time crime partner was severely wounded. The owner of the residence, Lee Davis, was arrested and transported to the Tulsa County jail.

Wilson, riddled with at least a dozen bullets was rushed to the Creek County jail for medical care and safekeeping. A crowd of over 500 citizens assembled at the jail that evening. When the throng began to get unruly, Sheriff Strange put out an SOS to Oklahoma Governor William Murray requesting help. Over 100 National Guardsmen showed up in short order, establishing a protective perimeter around the jail.

An uneasy night was passed at the Creek County facility where the huge mob had congregated hurling threats at the prisoner. An urgent call came into the police station around 2 a.m. reporting the sighting of Ford Bradshaw north of Sapulpa at an isolated farmhouse. Bradshaw had barley escaped capture in nearby Tulsa several days previous and was still thought to be in the area. Over a

Eldon Wilson killed at the Sapulpa shootout. Photo courtesy of the Muskogee-Times

Aussie Elliott killed at the Sapulpa shootout. Photo courtesy of the Sapulpa Herald.

dozen officers armed with machine guns and tear gas launched a raid on the residence. No gangsters were found. The information provided police turned out to be bogus, a case of an overactive imagination. Obviously, the city was on edge. About 8 a.m. Eldon Wilson, who had clung to life for nearly fifteen hours, died. The mass of angry citizens soon dispersed and the National Guardsmen were returned to Tulsa.

*****

An hour later and forty miles away in the small town of Chelsea, Oklahoma, Rogers County Deputy Sheriff Albert Powell and Town Constable Bud Roberts were touring the town on a peaceful Sunday morning when

Special Officer Floyd Sellers, Sheriff Willis Strange, and Deputy Wesley Gage. Photo courtesy of the Sapulpa Herald.

they spotted two men standing behind the Britt hardware store. Thinking they were a couple of farm boys hung over from a night on the town, the officers turned their cruiser around and drove up to the pair. Constable Roberts later stated, "The strangers began walking towards us, stopping about five feet from the car. Suddenly the men pulled out pistols and began firing point blank at me and Powell."

Powell, who had his gun in his lap returned fire, but was struck in the neck, and died instantly. According to Roberts, Powell fell onto him causing him to roll out on the pavement on the passenger side of the car. The mortally wounded Deputy's foot slipped off the clutch and the car rolled forward a few hundred feet, stopping when it hit a light pole. Roberts claimed he then pulled his gun and traded shots with the gunmen while he was fleeing towards a nearby drugstore to call for reinforcements. He also stated he didn't know which of the gunmen killed his partner. According to Paul Merritt, an elderly Chelsea native who witnessed the shootout when he was ten years old, "The officers pulled up to the hardware store where the men stood and both parties began firing at about the same time. Then Powell's car rolled down the street a block coming to an abrupt stop."

The streets of Chelsea circa 1930s. Photo courtesy of the Rogers County Historical Society

Deputies soon arrived from nearby Claremore. Lawmen encircled the hardware store and nearby lumberyard, carefully approaching the buildings. Powell's body was found nearby still laying in the front seat of his car. About 150 feet from Powell the officers spied another man who was shot in the chest, obviously dead. The man was identified by police and people in the assembling crowd as Eddie "Newt" Clanton "a local boy gone bad."

Examining Clanton's body up close, Rogers County Sheriff Faulkner claimed a small-caliber weapon had been used to shoot him. Officers Powell and Roberts carried large-caliber weapons. He observed powder burns on Clanton's shirt, indicating a contact wound.

The double killing in Chelsea was surrounded in mystery. The coroner stated a .32 caliber slug killed Clanton. Both lawmen carried .45 calibers that day. He also noted the powder burns on Clanton's shirt, indicating he was shot at very close range. Sherrif Faulkner concluded the second suspect with Clanton at the scene of the shooting shot his companion to steal his money. Clanton's brother, who lived four miles north of Chelsea, had since come forward claiming Newt had in his possession some $2,700 when he was seen with two unnamed companions the day before.

If the second man did kill Clanton, and that's a big if, maybe a clue lies in Clanton's past behavior. As was demonstrated earlier in this story, Clanton had little taste for gunplay and had stopped Wilber Underhill from killing two different times. Perhaps he tried to stop his companion from shooting the fleeing Constable Bud Roberts, and the two gunmen struggled, creating an accident. Remember, Chelsea was Clanton's hometown, and not a large community. He probably knew both officers. This seems a more likely scenario than Sheriff Faulkner's theory.

The outlaw's car was found wrecked three blocks away, loaded down with guns and ammunition. The officers surmised they were burglarizing the hardware store for more firearms.

Later that day Roy Dye, a local farm boy, called home telling a tale of terror to his family. Dye, who was taking a leisurely drive with young Lorene Rush, said that shortly after the shooting a man flagged down his car on the edge of town. The hijacker stuck a gun in his face and told him to drive north of town to the home of Clanton's brother, located in nearby Catale. When they arrived at the home the desperado stepped out of the car, took the keys, strode up to the house, and informed Clanton where he could find his brother's body. When the man returned to the stolen car, he flopped down in the passenger seat and informed Dye to drive the girl to her house. After releasing the woman with the admonition to keep her mouth shut or he'd come back and silence her permanently, the kidnapper had Dye drive him to Fort Smith, Arkansas, where he released the boy and handed him a five-dollar bill for his trouble. Dye initially identified his kidnapper as Ford Bradshaw. The boy's car was recovered a week later in downtown Vian being driven by Charlie Cotner's wife. His two sisters were passengers in the rig. All were arrested and later released by authorities.

Lawmen believed that Dye was correct in his identification. They suspected both Bradshaw and Charlie Cotner were present at the Chelsea shootout when their partner was killed. The pair recently had been spotted in nearby Tulsa, and at the Clanton farm the day before the shootout. It was believed Cotner was either standing in the darkened door of the hardware store, or sitting in the getaway car a half a block away at the time of the shooting. Officers assumed the pair separated after they wrecked the car while trying to flee the scene of the crime. The identification of the suspects cast suspicion on the police theory implying Clanton's partner cold bloodedly murdered him for the money he was carrying. Say what you may about Bradshaw's violent ways, but according to numerous sources he was as close as a brother to Clanton. It seems unlikely that he murdered his nephew-in-law and long-time partner. As to the second suspect, Cotner was known as a thief, not a killer. Soon after the shootout, a rumor surfaced implying the lawmen had stolen the $2,700 and made up the story of Clanton's death being caused by a smaller caliber bullet.

His father, who managed a café in nearby Vinita, claimed the body of twenty-six year-old Edward "Newt" Clanton, sometimes known as "Little Joe." He was buried in Chelsea's Snyder Cemetery. Sheriff Cannon of Muskogee expressed satisfaction with Clanton's demise, saying he had carried in his cruiser for nearly two years a pair of warrants for suspicion of murder in the Sharp case which he intended to serve on Clanton and Bradshaw whenever they were captured. With the death of Clanton, only one of the main suspects in the Sharp murder remained at large.

A few days after the Powell murder, the US Attorney's office met in secret to consider filing Federal-kidnapping charges against Bradshaw. This would have been only the second time in Oklahoma history that federal authorities had used the so-called "Lindbergh Law," which provided for the death penalty. The Rogers County District Attorney stated he would seek at the next meeting of the Grand Jury murder charges against Bradshaw, and a charge of accessory to murder against Cotner for the death of Deputy Powell. Although authorities at first thought Clanton killed Deputy Powell, the general opinion of many of the investigators after reviewing the evidence, considered Ford Bradshaw the prime suspect in his murder.

The following day Deputy Albert Pike Powell, who was survived by a wife and seven children, was given the heroes funeral he deserved. He had been a resident of Chelsea for some thirty-five years and had also been the fire chief of the small town. The Deputy had been a well-loved and respected member of the community. He was interred at the Chelsea Cemetery. Powell was the second Rogers County deputy to die at the hands of the Cookson Hills Gang, the first being Deputy Hurt Flippen in the 1932 Cherokee County shootout with "Kye" Carlile and Troy Love. Federal Officials quickly launched an investigation to ascertain if the shootouts in Chelsea and Sapulpa had any connection. It was suspected by authorities at the time that if there was a link between the two outlaw groups it was through Aussie Elliott, one of those killed in the Sapulpa raid. He was noted by lawmen as a known associate and pal of several members of the Cookson Hills bunch.

Clyde Barrow. Photo courtesy of the Joplin-Globe

But it was never proven there was anything connecting the actions of the two groups on that deadly weekend. Bradshaw and Cotner now joined ranks with the likes of Charlie Floyd and Clyde Barrow as two of the most wanted men in the Midwest.

******

Charles Floyd. Photo courtesy of True Detective Magazine

O. P. Ray, head of Oklahoma's Department of Criminal Investigation decided along with Major Wint Smith, commander of the Kansas Highway Patrol he'd had enough of the Cookson Hills and its bandits. Lawmen had been thwarted by the residents of the Hills who were continually uncooperative and had actively hid out outlaws for several years during the height of the current Midwest crime wave. Kansas authorities bemoaned the fact their state was undergoing an epidemic of bank robberies, perpetrated by outlaws who committed a crime in the state then fleeing back to their hideouts in the Cooksons where the locals harbored them. After an intensive investigation, Kansas lawmen realized the Hills had become a recruiting depot for young men hired by the Bradshaws and others to drive get-away cars and act as lookouts in hold ups in their state. As the depression deepened, bank robbery had become a cottage industry in the Cooksons. There certainly were no jobs or business opportunities lying around. To be offered a couple of hundred dollars for a quick trip to Kansas would have been a great temptation to a young man, especially when $200 amounted to a king's ransom in those days. Officers, with the encouragement of Governors Murray of Oklahoma, and Landon of Kansas, began formulating a plan to raid the hills in a big way.

In February 1934, law enforcement officers from both states, with the assistance of a contingent of US Department of Justice officers led by senior agent Frank Smith, began an assault on the Hills and their criminal element. Over 400 lawmen from nearly every county in Oklahoma, supplemented by a large contingent from Kansas, assembled at points around the Cooksons on the evening of February 16. O. P. Ray the head of Oklahoma Bureau of Investigation was disgusted when he heard from his sources that word had leaked out of the huge raid. He requested local newspapers to run stories of how the event had been cancelled, which they did the next day.

On the cold drizzling morning of February 17 officers struck, setting up roadblocks at every settlement and crossroads in the hill country. Their stated prey was Charlie

The National Guard in the Cookson Raid. Photo courtesy of True Detective Magazine

Floyd who hadn't been seen in the area for several months and Ford Bradshaw, along with his sidekick Charlie Cotner. Authorities had also gotten word that the Barrow Gang from Texas might also be in the hills. Clyde Barrow, along with his girlfriend, Bonnie Parker, and several others were a pack of kill-crazy Texas hoodlums who had terrorized the Midwest for over a year. The deadly and elusive Barrow was wanted for numerous murders and small-time robberies, including the death of an Oklahoma officer near Stringtown. The gang had been known to drift into the hills to hide now and then.

The next day, over 300 Oklahoma national guardsmen from Muskogee, Wagoner, Tahlequah, Tulsa, and elsewhere were called out to assist the lawmen. Several times officers manning roadblocks shot out tires of fleeing hoodlums. The only casualty reported was Coalgate Chief of Police Bill Jones who was wounded in both legs by several shotgun pellets when a fellow officer accidentally discharged his weapon. Eighteen people were arrested that weekend, including Luther Jolliff, the missing witness in

The officers of the Cookson Hill raid flushing out the criminals.
Photo courtesy of True Detective Magazine

the Sharp murder case. Also detained were Bradshaw's brother Kerman of rural Bunch, his sister Rema, niece Ruth Clanton, and seventeen-year-old nephew Duester Huggins. They were all hauled into Muskogee for questioning. But the big boys like Floyd and Bradshaw were not seen, although Oklahoma County Sheriff Stanley Rogers was quoted as saying that the posse had only missed Bradshaw by a "hairs breath" in his opinion. The raid, one of the largest in US history, may have had a psychological effect on the residents but it achieved little.

The week after the raid there was a flurry of letters printed in several local newspapers protesting the push into the hills. Most of the residents of the Cooksons were of the opinion that the sweep was a publicity stunt. George Stratton, the owner of the store in the village of Cookson, decried that the officers didn't accomplish a thing; he called it a waste of time and taxpayers' money. A Reverend Thelmer of Muskogee wrote that the cost of the operation could of fed every starving child in the Hills for a month. He claimed that poverty, not criminals, was the root problem in the district. A county commissioner stated that money was needed for roads, not raids. He claimed that a good road through the hills would end the isolated existence of the residents, and bring in tourists and sportsmen, instead of outlaws.

Chapter 10

The End of the Line

In the early morning hours of March 3, 1934, Laflore County and Fort Smith city officers received a riot call concerning a roadhouse just inside the Oklahoma border near Arkoma. Several carloads of officers, from both departments, loaded up with shotguns and tear gas speeding to the site. The club's manager, Bob Harper, met officers on their arrival. His brother Bill Harper, a part time (auxiliary) Laflore County deputy sheriff, owned the establishment. Bob Harper told officers that a man accompanied by a woman had held the customers of the nightclub hostage for several hours, robbing and threatening his fellow partygoers with a .45 caliber pistol. It was later ascertained, the man was angry over the loss of a $100 at an illegal gaming table in the place. The manager also stated the individual went on a rampage destroying all the slot machines in the juke joint. Harper eventually slipped out of the tavern unnoticed and called authorities.

Ford Bradshaw. Photo courtesy of the Muskogee-Times

Two Sebastian County deputy sheriffs, Prentece Maddux and Lew Williams, entered the back door of the establishment armed with sawed-off shotguns. The officers soon spotted the rowdy customer finishing off another slot machine with a baseball bat. A command of "Put em up, bud," was issued and the bad man hesitantly complied. The man's female companion, who deputies later described as a "good looking gal, wearing a cowboy hat," was also corralled by the lawmen.

The hell raiser was forced to disarm and take off a bulletproof vest he was wearing. The suspect was handcuffed. Harper's brother, Bill, soon arrived and he and the Arkansas officers led the suspect outside towards a patrol car. Suddenly, the man struck Bill Harper in the face and bolted towards the door knocking over the Sebastian County officers in the process. Bill Harper jacked a round into his Colt .45 and put three slugs into the fleeing man's back. The man fell to the ground just outside the back door, rolling over on his back. When he saw Harper taking aim at his chest, he cried, "Don't do that," as the Deputy fired two more bullets into his body.

The woman who had been his companion ran towards the man crying "Oh Daddy." She also screamed at Harper, "I'll see that you get yours, chump." The woman was ar-

Front page of the McAlester News-Capital March 4, 1934.

rested for drunkenness. When questioned by officers she claimed her name was Mary Jane Fields. At first she refused to tell lawmen who her slain companion was, then proclaimed that he was Clyde Barrow and she Bonnie Parker. Officers doubted her truthfulness and told her so. An hour or so later the woman spoke up again telling the

Front page of the Muskogee-Times Democrat March 3, 1934.

officers that, "The man's plenty hot, wait tell you finger-print him, you'll see he's plenty wanted too." Laflore County lawmen took his prints, but a look at the wanted posters back at the Sheriffs office convinced them the dead man was Ford Bradshaw. The Sheriff called the Muskogee County Sheriffs department, asking them to send some-one over to help identify the outlaw. Deputy Cash Russ responded. One look at the slain man and Russ immedi-ately confirmed that it was indeed the infamous gunman. Mary Jane Fields turned out to be Stella "Boots" Moody, Bradshaw's long-lost girlfriend. She had been sought by lawmen to testify in the 1932 Martin murder case in Muskogee in which her boyfriend was the chief suspect.

A search of Bradshaw's car, a new Chevy (Ford only drove Chevys) turned up over a 100 rounds of ammuni-tion, a sawed-off automatic shotgun, two pistols, a rifle, and luggage. A manila envelope containing numerous let-ters was also found in the search. One piece of unfinished correspondence written on a Kansas City hotel's letter-head by Miss Moody to a friend wrote about her and Bradshaw having some sort of recent encounter with Clyde Barrow and Bonnie Parker.

The following day several Oklahoma and Arkansas newspapers reported the outlaw's demise in blazing head-lines. Papers in Nebraska, Arkansas, Missouri, and Kan-sas also noted his death. The Harper brothers were quoted, making a great deal of self-serving statements. Bill Harper, who by shooting the handcuffed and unarmed Bradshaw in the back, as well as operating an illegal gambling den while serving as a peace officer, knew that he was skating on thin ice legally. He asserted that the fleeing Bradshaw was trying to make it to his car to grab a shotgun that was found on the front seat. Bill's brother, Bob Harper the inn-keeper, stated he could have taken the bandit out anytime during the siege, but didn't want the man's murder on his conscience. He also blowed off, that the outlaw was "Just a punk." It is doubtful he expressed this sentiment to Bradshaw while he was alive. Within hours of the shooting the two Arkansas officers dragged Bill Harper in front of a local magistrate who charged him with suspicion of murder and set a date for a hearing in front of the county Judge. It seems the officers agreed with the idea that Bradshaw needed killing, but were uncomfortable about the way it was done.

Law enforcement officials were overjoyed at the report of the outlaw's death. A spokesman for the US Department of Justice, the forerunner of the FBI, said he welcomed the outlaw's demise. He stated the bandit was a "violent thug of the first order, and one of the worst cold blooded killers in the nation." Muskogee County Sheriff V. S. Cannon was quoted as saying "I'm glad they got him; he was a bad apple." John Johnson, the agent from the Oklahoma Bureau of Investigation who arrested Bradshaw for the first time in 1928, was quoted as saying, "He was what you'd call a jellybean bandit, a ladies man, but a real smart aleck, he was mean and would shoot 'ya if you got in his way." Lawmen also stated that at the time of his demise, the bandit was a prime suspect in five murder investigations and ten armed robberies. The best that can be said about Bradshaw is that he lived a wasted life. With the death of Ford Bradshaw at the age of twenty-eight, all of Susie Sharp's killers were either dead or incarcerated.

The following day Sunday, March 4, the bandit's body was transported from the Poteau morgue to Moores Funeral home in Sallisaw. The Harper's roadhouse windows were broken out and the brothers soon began receiving death threats.

The next day Ford's body was moved to the Bradshaw

home, seven miles northeast of Vian. Over 1,200 people had viewed the body at the funeral home and another 1,500 came to the Bradshaw cabin to pass by his casket, which sat in the breezeway. Reporters stated that Bradshaw's childhood sweetheart, Blanche Cotner, wept openly at the foot of the outlaw's coffin. "Boots" Moody, who had been released by the authorities, was not seen. A request by the family to have the incarcerated "Skeet" attend the funeral was denied by Sheriff Cannon citing security reasons. That evening, lawmen escorted a group of bankers from Baxter Springs, Wellington, and Galena, Kansas, to view the body to try to identify Bradshaw as one of the bandits who had robbed their institutions. They all made positive identifications.

The funeral was held at the home that day as the crowd sang "I'll Fly Away," Ford's favorite song. Incidentally, Bradshaw was reported to have had a fine singing voice. Reverend George Mitchell of Sallisaw preached the funeral, telling the crowd that Bradshaw had been gunned down like a dog by the Harpers and not given a fair chance. This incited a great deal of talk by the locals about extracting revenge on the brothers. Sequoyah County flower shop owners reported they received so many orders for wreaths they sold out and referred customers to flower shops in Fort Smith and Muskogee.

About 3 p.m. a hearse loaded up the body for the quarter-mile trip to the family cemetery located behind the house in a small valley. In a strange turn of events, instead of turning down the dirt lane to the cemetery, the hearse raced towards Muskogee. On arrival in the city, the hearse drove up to the front door of the County Jail where a corridor of officers surrounded it. Sheriff Cannon had agreed at the last moment to allow "Skeet" to pay his final respects to his brother. The prisoner was led out to the hearse manacled to deputies where he kissed his young wife, hugged his mother, and then peered into the open casket to view his slain brother. Reporters said the young man showed no emotion.

"Skeet" was allowed a few minutes then hauled back into the jail. The hearse sped off towards the hills. Reporters had been told that because of the late hour, Bradshaw would be buried the next morning. However, on the trip back to the cemetery, the family changed their minds due to an old hill superstition that a grave, when opened, must be filled in on the same day. At nearly nine, that evening the handsome bandit's mortal remains were lowered into the earth as the misty-eyed crowd sang "Amazing Grace." Witnesses told of it being an eerie event. It was a dark moonless night with only the headlights of several cars illuminating the scene.

Bill Harper was given a hearing on the charge of murdering Bradshaw the following Tuesday in Poteau. At the hearing, the Bradshaw family lawyer requested, at the insistence of the Mother, Mary Bradshaw, in what could be described as an act of charity, that all charges against the Harpers be dropped. The lawyer, A. M. Degraffenreid, stated that although the Bradshaw family had no sympathy for Harper, the mother wanted the nightmare to end, as she didn't look forward to a lengthy trial of Harper. Mary Bradshaw also made a public statement through her lawyer that she wanted no reprisals against the Harpers; she stated that enough killings had occurred. She needn't have worried. Judge Flanagan replied he didn't care what Mother Bradshaw thought and dismissed all charges against Harper saying no court in the land would convict him for killing a rat like Bradshaw. The judge did revoke Harpers liquor license.

At the same hearing the Bradshaw sisters asked for

the return of the car Ford was driving and the $400 of stolen money they claimed he was carrying when they saw the bandit the night before his death at the Bradshaw cabin. The Judge laughed at that one too. Incidentally, the money was never accounted for. A red-faced "Boots" Moody showed up at the hearing. She sat in the front row silently glaring at Bill Harper throughout the entire inquest.

When interviewed later that day, the Bradshaw family told reporters Ford had been tipped off days before the impending massive Cookson Hills raid which occurred on February 17 and 18. They also claimed he had been living in a rented apartment in Carthage, Missouri, with Miss Moody for the past two or three weeks. When lawmen checked out the Carthage story, authorities there replied that Bradshaw's sweetheart, Miss Moody, using her alias, Mary Jane Fields, had been released from the Carthage city jail only the day before his death. It seems that Carthage police and sheriff's officers had raided the apartment where Bradshaw, Moody, and Charlie Cotner were living the previous week. The trio was suspected by lawmen to be the same two masked men and a woman who had robbed the First National Bank of Galena, Kansas, on February 24 of $7,100. This was the second time the pair was suspected of robbing the same Galena bank. Authorities also suspected members of the Barrow gang had committed the robbery; they were thought to have been in the three-state corners area during that time. Police captured Moody, but missed Bradshaw and his pal, who weren't home at the time of the raid. She was held several days for suspicion before being released.

******

At dawn, March 15, twenty-eight Federal, Oklahoma and Kansas lawmen raided a small four-room farmhouse belonging to Ira Brackett near Mannford, Oklahoma. Federal officers had received a tip that several members of the notorious Barker Gang were hiding at the house. The Department of Justice had been conducting a nationwide search for the kidnappers of Edward Bremer in Minneapolis, Minnesota. Bremer had been taken in January 1934 and released after a ransom of $200,000 was paid in February. Soon afterwards the fingerprints of Dock Barker was found on a gas can and flashlight connected

Dock Barker. Courtesy of the Oklahoma Department of Corrections and Naomi Morgan

to the crime. Barker was a known member of the so-called Barker-Karpis Gang, which included members Fred and Dock Barker, Alvin Karpis, Larry DeVol, Harry Campbell, and many others. The gang had terrorized the Midwest since their beginnings in Tulsa, Oklahoma, in the early 1920s. The group at times numbered as many as thirty members and associates that committed numerous robberies and kidnappings, evolving

Alvin Karpis. Photo courtesy of Mike Koch.

into the first and largest of the 1930s super gangs.

The tip the Feds had received involved the suspected presence of Harry Campbell and Glenn Roy Wright, both known members of the Barker Gang. The two men were suspected of involvement in the Bremer snatch, and a robbery of a farm auction in Payne County, Oklahoma, that netted the thieves $5,000. They were also wanted for questioning about the August 18,1933, murder of Tulsa attorney J. Earle Smith. The lawyer was an alleged crony of the Barker

Charlie Cotner.
Photo courtesy of the
Muskogee-Times

gang who was hired by them to represent Harvey Bailey, an associate of the Barkers, at a court hearing. The attorney pulled a no show, and it appears the gang members killed him for his forgetfulness. In addition to the Smith killing, Wright was wanted in Miami, Oklahoma, for the fatal shooting of William Witten who was killed during a robbery in Picher, Oklahoma, in May 1933.

Newly appointed Sapulpa Chief of Police Floyd Sellers led the raid by kicking in the front door. Sellers recently had been involved in the shootout at Lee Davis' farm near Sapulpa, Oklahoma, where two lawmen and three suspects had been killed. Eight persons were nabbed in the Mannford raid, where none offered resistance. It was reported that all the suspects were in various stages of undress.

Officers identified the captured suspects as Glen Roy Wright, Charlie Cotner, Frank Downey, Ed Brophy, and J. W. McAtee who was assumed to be Harry Campbell. Two women were also apprehended. Their names were given as Grace Cutler, who later turned out to be Ruby Cotner, Charlie's wife, and Winnie Morris, which proved to be another alias for the twenty-year-old Stella "Boots" Moody, Ford Bradshaw's girlfriend who was with him when he was killed. A dozen open safes from banks in a three-state area were found on the premises. Also seized was a full box of syringes, a vial of morphine, several counterfeit twenty-dollar bills, and two quarts of nitro glycerin.

Glenn Roy Wright. Photo courtesy of the Muskogee-Times

McAtee later proved not to be Campbell, to the great disappointment of the Feds, but they were still very pleased to catch Wright and Charlie Cotner, who had been Ford Bradshaw's right hand man until his death, and

John McAtee. Photo courtesy of the Muskogee-Times.

was probably the new leader of what was left of the gang. Cotner was wanted for questioning in fifteen Kansas and Arkansas bank robberies and burglaries. Oklahoma authorities also wanted him for his suspected complicity in the murder of Deputy Sheriff Albert Powell in Chelsea. Kansas lawmen wanted to question him about the alleged kidnapping scheme involving Governor Alf Landon's daughter. The five men were rushed to the Oklahoma State Prison in McAlester for safekeeping.

Sequoyah County authorities later expressed interest in questioning Cotner about the incident in Vian, where allegedly he, Bradshaw, and Wilbur Underhill terrorized the town for several hours. He was a man in great demand.

******

The following day Robert Trollinger was arrested at a roadhouse near Willow Springs, Missouri, by a posse led by Texas County Sheriff A. P. Johnson. Trollinger had long been a member of the Cookson Hills gang. Sheriff Virgil Cannon had always suspected Trollinger as the third man involved in the gunfight at Standing Rock, where Deputy Walter Reese and Tahlequah Policeman Frank Edwards were killed, although his theory was never proven. Trollinger was also wanted by Nebraska lawmen for the York Bank robbery and Arkansas authorities for questioning for his suspected involvement in bank robberies in Mansfield and Fayetteville. Kansas lawmen also sought the outlaw for his alleged presence at several robberies in the "Sunflower" state.

Bankers from Galena and Baxter Springs, Kansas, positively identified Cotner as being present at the robberies of both institutions. Kansas authorities asked for his extradition to their state to be tried for these robberies. Oklahoma hedged on the idea at first, hoping to try him for complicity in Deputy Powell's murder in Chelsea. Roy Dye, the kidnap victim in the Chelsea incident who had at first identified Bradshaw as his captor, then had second thoughts, was brought forward to identify Cotner as his hijacker. Dye stated Cotner was definitely not the man who had kidnapped him. After Dye's failure to identify Cotner, Oklahoma authorities allowed Kansas to extradite the bandit.

On April 20, officers in Fayetteville, Arkansas, arrested Mount Cookson, who surrendered peacefully. Cookson, who was known as an independent operator, was probably never a full time member of the Bradshaw gang, but was suspected of committing a robbery or two with them. He was wanted for his suspected participation in the robberies of the Midland and Mansfield, Arkansas, banks, as well as others. The forty-six year old bandit was later convicted of the Mansfield job on September 27, 1934, and sentenced to fifteen years confinement as inmate #33011.

On May 18 Cotner pled not guilty to the October 30, 1933, Galena, Kansas, bank robbery. The bankers and customers who witnessed the robbery all identified him as one of the perpetrators of the crime. When the bandit was questioned he swore to the officers he had never stepped foot on Kansas soil, then glaring at the Sheriff, added, "before you law dogs hauled me here." Muskogee County Deputy Bob Ledbetter testified that Curtis Hammond, a Vian constable and longtime acquaintance of Cotners, told him and other investigators that Cotner stated to him in a conversation, that he and Bradshaw with the help of others had robbed the Galena Bank. Hammond was called to the stand. The Constable denied the conversation. He even went further, stating he had seen Cotner the day of the Galena robbery in Vian. The Kansas Judge charged Hammond with perjury.

The jury found Cotner guilty. The errant bank robber was initially sentenced to ten to fifty years in the Kansas State Prison. The following day, Cherokee County, Kansas, Judge John W. Hamilton resentenced Cotner to twenty to one hundred years, due to the fact that he had previously served a term in the Arkansas State Prison for armed robbery. Under Kansas law this fact made him a habitual offender, thus doubling his sentence. The Vian constable who tried to alibi Cotner was tried for perjury in January of 1935. Three deputy sheriffs and a US marshal testified against him in open court. All four claimed that the talkative peace officer had relayed to them that Cotner admitted to the constable he and Bradshaw were guilty of the Galena robbery. The trial ended in a hung jury. Around this time, Glenn Leroy Wright was also found guilty for armed robbery and was sentenced to McAlester for life. He died in prison in 1954. Cotners wife and "Boots" Moody, who appeared to be a classic starstruck gangster moll of the period, were let loose after a few days in the calaboose and a lecture in which the judge told them basically to go and sin no more. The Cookson Hill-Bradshaw-Underhill gang was loosing steam and members fast.

******

On April 25, Ford Bradshaw's nephew, Duester Huggins, and Blanche Cotner's companion, Dr. Cecil Bryan, were involved in a nasty car accident three miles south of Keefton, Oklahoma. According to witnesses, the Bryan car slammed into a vehicle belonging to a man named Crawford that was disabled on the side of the road. Apparently Bryan had fallen asleep at the wheel; his car rear-ended the Crawford truck which was loaded down with eggs, cream, and chickens going to market in nearby Sallisaw. The doctor was badly injured. The Huggins boy, who was unscratched, jumped out of the wrecked car and began threatening Crawford and several passengers who were along for the ride. He announced to the crowd, assembled at the site of the accident that they better not mess with him, cause he was one of the Bradshaw bunch. An ambulance soon arrived transporting Bryan to the Baptist

Hospital in Muskogee. Huggins hopped a ride in the ambulance. On his arrival at the hospital, he was met and interviewed by Deputy Bob Ledbetter. It was reported that the young man was uncooperative and still making threats towards Crawford in the presence of the deputy, who arrested him for drunkenness. After handcuffing the lad, Ledbetter searched him and found a pistol in his pocket. Huggins was transported to the county jail where he joined his Uncle "Skeet." Charges were later dropped and Duester released. A month later, he was killed in a bizarre automobile accident.

******

Meanwhile "Skeet" Bradshaw's lawyer, A. M. Degraffenreid, filed for a change of venue. District Judge F.A. Summers refused the request. Several days later on May 2, attorneys for Jim Benge also asked for a change of venue, and this request was denied. A somber faced Thomas "Skeet" Bradshaw stood before the bench of Judge Summers on May 5, 1934 to plea guilty to the attempted murder of Charles Green of Webber Falls, Oklahoma. His lawyer had worked out a plea bargain which stated several other charges against him would be dismissed and any time given him having to do with the Federal whiskey charges would be served concurrently with the state charges. The judge sentenced Bradshaw to five years in the Oklahoma State Prison, and delivered to him a lecture. Bradshaw was told that he was young enough to serve his time and still become a productive citizen. He was transferred to the State Prison in McAlester on May 7 as inmate #29768.

******

On a lighter note, on the evening of May 22, 1934, Owen Sharp, the surviving son of Susie Sharp, was enjoying the company of several friends stretched out near a blazing fire on the banks of the Illinois River. They were soon joined by a group of three off-duty Muskogee County deputies who were also on a weekend fishing jaunt. By all accounts the group was having good luck, catching some fair sized catfish, when from out of the darkness someone shouted "hands up." The campers thought it was a joke; until they saw two men armed with pistols approach the fire. The bandits robbed the group of not only their money, but also fishing equitment, guns, watches, jewlry, tents and even the fish they had on their stringers. The outlaws threw the plunder into the deputies' car, after disabling Owen Sharp's rig, and sped off. The embarrassed lawmen walked to the town of Gore and called for help. By the time other officers could get to the campsite, the bandits had melted into the vastness of the Cooksons.

******

On May 8 the case of the State of Oklahoma vs. Jim Benge began for the murder of Susie Sharp in Muskogee District court. Several witnesses were called, including Luther Jolliff, Ben Parnell and his wife, and Pearl Anderson, Susie Sharp's daughter who had been shot in the back by the killers. Elias Sharp, Susie's husband, attended the trial every day sitting in the front row. Benge was defended by Harry Pitchford, the same lawyer who had represented Bradshaw in his trial for robbing the bank in Henryetta in which he was aquitted. The only excitement occurred when Pitchford lost his temper when the district attorney called his client a "Jaybird," a term which Benge's lawyer took offense. Jolliff testified (unwillingly I might add) that he had eaten dinner with Carlile, Love, Benge, and two men known to him as "Slim" and "Shorty" the afternoon of the murder at Ben Parnell's house. He also testified that later in the early part of the evening he drove the men to a spot near Braggs Mountain and then drove up the hill to buy a dozen hamburgers for the group. After bringing back the food, he drove back home. Jolliff also testified he never saw Benge with a weapon, nor did he think the big Indian or any of the others in the group were capable of killing a woman. Defendant Benge sat expressionless and still as a stone during his testimony. Parnell's testimony dovetailed Jolliff's, except for the fact he and his wife identified the mug shots they viewed of Ford Bradshaw and Ed Clanton as greatly resembling the men introduced to them the day of the murder as "Slim" and "Shorty." He further stated that after lunch, the men took target practice behind his house with a variety of weapons.

A great deal of circumstantial evidence was also submitted by the state against the defendant. The case went to the jury on May 10. A few days later, the jury came in with a verdict of guilty and suggested life imprisonment. Several jury members said there was no doubt in their minds that Benge was guilty, but they didn't think he pulled the trigger, thus they didn't have the heart to send the handsome bandit to the electric chair.

On May 29, Judge Summers in his remarks before sentencing Benge commented on the heinous nature of the crime, saying the five men on that mountainside in 1932 were all career criminals who meant harm. He sited the fact that they were "liquored up and became excited when a car came driving up the mountain, which they intended on stealing." He added, "In their excitement they shot at the car when it wouldn't stop." He stated that by law, all the men involved were technically guilty of the murder of

Sharp. He also commented that from the original five suspects and their associates, a host of other crimes had been committed over the past two years. The judge went on to call the gang, "a cancer on society." He sited the fact not only were four of the suspects killed by gunfire, numerous lawmen had died in the pursuit of these men and their associates. He also stated the case against Benge was so strong they could try him forty times and the only differnce in the outcome would be whether he got life in prison or death. Summers then sentenced Benge to life imprisonment saying he regretted it had not been the electric chair. Benge entered the Oklahoma State Prison on May 30 as inmate #29885. He was the only person ever convicted in the Sharp murder case.

Luther Jolliff came to trial in June 1934. Since he had reluctantly cooperated in the States case against Benge, all state charges had been dropped in his case. It has long been suspected the authorities had threatend him with a murder charge if he didn't testify against Benge. Ironically, it was a charge he was obviously innocent of. He plead guilty to a federal charge of illegal possession of liquor and was sentenced to six months at El Reno Federal Detention Center.

******

On October 22, 1934, the infamous "Pretty Boy" Floyd, the so-called "Robin Hood of the Cookson Hills," was shot down near East Liverpool, Ohio, by FBI agents led by Melvin Purvis. Over 30,000 mostly rural poor citizens attended his funeral near Akins, Oklahoma. In the few short years of his career as a bandit, he had become a folk hero to many people of the state. Poor dirt farmers who had lost their land through bank foreclosures or just families who had hit rock bottom felt that every time he robbed a bank he stuck a blow for the common folk against the rich, who many blamed for the depression.

******

The final nail in the gang's coffin came on November 25, 1934, when Adair and Sequoyah County lawmen, aided by Kansas State police officers, captured Hunter Cotner, brother of Charlie, and his two companions, Ira Clark and Evan Bass. The Kansas Attorney General's office said that Cotner was the last link in a chain of some fifteen outlaws of the so called "Cookson Hills" gang who had participated in the robbery and burglaries of more than two dozen banks and businesses in the three-state area. Cotner was spirited to McPherson, Kansas, where he pled guilty to the robbery of the Windom State Bank. He was sentenced to two five-year terms at the Kansas State Prison in Lansing. His pals, Clark and Bass, along with Cotner were also suspects in two other bank robberies, one in Gravette, Arkansas, and another in Honeywell, Kansas. With Hunter Cotner's, arrest the gang as an active unit was finished.

J. Edgar Hoover. Photo courtesy of the Springfield News and Leader

Did the Cookson Hills gang commit all the robberies of which they were suspected? Probably not. Like another Hills badman, Charlie Floyd, once they were well known they were accused of virtually every crime committed in the tri-state area. But, like Floyd, they certainly committed their share. Members of the gang were suspected in many more robberies than are noted in this book, such as the banks of Red Cloud and Kearney, Nebraska, Weir and Leroy, Kansas, England, Arkansas, and others. The group was also connected to ten incidents of violent death. In human terms, that is ten widows and God knows how many fatherless children left to fend for themselves in the midst of the depression. Another question is, "who was the gang's leader?" The answer also depends on the time. Early on, it seems that "Kye" Carlile certainly was the driving force; later Ford Bradshaw; and, for a time it seems Wilber Underhill shared the helm with Bradshaw. After the pair's deaths, Charlie Cotner must have run the show.

House where Ma and son Freddy Barker were killed. Photo courtesy of the Springfield News and Leader

The big Midwest crime wave was ending by the mid 30s. Dillinger bit the dust in 1934. A posse in Louisiana shot Bonnie and Clyde to pieces in May of the same year. On January 16, 1935, Fred and Ma Barker were surrounded and killed by the FBI in Lake Weir, Florida. "Dock" Barker was killed attempting to escape from Alcatraz. As the big name gangs began disappearing, the public's fascination with criminals dwindled. But, for a few short years, the "Baby Face" Nelsons and "Pretty Boy" Floyds were the superstars of early radio and newspapers. I suppose the coverage of the bandits' adventures and the public's fascination of J. Edger Hoover, Melvin Purvis, and the G-Men took people's minds off the bone-crushing weariness of the depression.

Bonnie and Clyde death car. Photo courtesy of Springfield News and Leader AP-Photo

Chapter 11

Rema

The Cookson Hills gang may have been broken apart as an active unit by mid-1934, but there was more fire to come by family members and associates of the group. Around this time, newspapers reported the death of Charlie Dotson of tuburculosis. He had contracted the disease shortly after arriving at the Nebraska State Prison. In the early 1930s, there was a near epidemic of TB in the nation's crowded prisons. The policy of most correctional facilities in the depression era was for inmates diagnosed with the dread illness to be sent home to recover or die. States did not want to assume responsibility for medical costs involved in caring for inmates. In Dotson's case, his wife and her family begged Nebraska prison officials to release him. It was a request which was denied. His family de-

"Big Mac" circa around 1930s. Photo courtesy of the Oklahoma Department of Corrections

clared the little Indian should be released because he had caught the White Man's plague. Prison officials responded that the problem was the little Indian had also learned to rob the White Man's banks. Dotson gave up the ghost on June 5th, 1934. He is buried in the Dwight Mission graveyard near Marble City.

On June 26, 1936, a near blind and tubercular Skeet Bradshaw was released from the Oklahoma State Prison. He had spent many months in the dungeons there in complete darkness, most likely brutalized by a prison system that could be characterized as heartless at best. In the 1920s and '30s, the state pen in McAlester, dubbed "Big Mac" by the convicts, could have been described as unhealthy, overcrowded, brutal, and inhumane. It was still the days of hard labor, road gangs and the ball and chain. All who knew "Skeet" Bradshaw described him as being "double tough and a real hard case." It's a certainty that he presented a challenge to the guards when he arrived there. In defense of the prison, they had their hands full with overcrowding, meager state funding, and public indifference. The Oklahoma and Kansas State prisons were a depository for most of the extremely dangerous criminals of the Midwest crime wave of the 1930s.

Ball and chain used in the 1930s on display at the Oklahoma Department of Corrections Museum. Photo by Naomi Morgan.

Skeet arrived back to a family farm that was out of control. His mother, father, and brother were dead. His sister Rema, and her daughter, Ruth, another sister, Gypsy, and his wife, Lulu, occupied the farm. In the past couple of years the hilltop the house sat on had become known as "Widow Hill," because all the women residing there were widows or their men were in prison. Old timers describe the farm as a place noted for it's round-the-clock boisterous parties. It had become a hideout for every wanted man for miles around. It's doubtful, that a near-blind (he had to wear thick coke bottle glasses the remainder of his life), stooped-over, and broken-down "Skeet" could have calmed the place down if he had wanted to.

******

On the afternoon of Wednesday September 16, 1936, Sheriff Bill Byrd with Under Sheriff Raymond Drake were combing the hills near the Bradshaw farm, searching for Carl Janaway, an escapee from the Arkansas prison system. Janaway was described as a 90-pound runt, who was a suspect in several bank robberies and auto thefts. The posse, with the aide of bloodhounds, including "Old Boston," the legendary tracking hound owned by the state, eventually trailed the outlaw to the back door of the Bradshaw home. It was rumored that he had been sparking Rema at

Deputy Raymond Drake. Photo courtesy of the Drake family.

night and spending his days hiding in the thick timber.

The lawmen approached the house, calling for its occupants to come out with their hands up. Suddenly Janaway and a companion bolted out the back door firing guns. Deputy Drake was struck in the right arm with a full load of buckshot from Janaway's shotgun. The blast literally shredded the bone and muscles in his arm. Janaway made his escape unhurt but his companion, Fred Luna, was wounded and captured.

The next day, nearly one hundred citizens and lawmen, including newly elected Sheriff Tom Jordan and a contingent of Muskogee County officers, gathered in Sallisaw and set off on a two-week pursuit of the slippery Janaway. It has been said the bandit hid in or near the Dwight Mission and it's cemetery, where some locals brought him food. He eventually stole the car of a fisherman on the Illinois River and fled the area.

Janaway was later caught in Saint Louis and sentenced to federal prison where he served five years in Alcatraz and then six more at the Federal Medical Center in Springfield, Missouri. Like so many inmates he contracted TB; but in his case he was not released due to a Federal policy of providing medical care for tubercular inmates instead of sending them back to their families. When he was released from federal custody in 1944, Oklahoma authorities were waiting at the prison gates to take him back to the "Sooner State" to be tried for the assault on Raymond Drake. Janaway was quickly found guilty of attempted murder and given a sentence of ten years. He was received at the Oklahoma State Prison as inmate #46639 on October 16 1945.

******

In early October 1936, angry lawmen who'd had enough of the Bradshaw place and it's occupants arrested seven people at the residence. These included Rema Deetjen, Ruth Clanton, "Skeet," and Lulu, his wife, on a charge of harboring criminals. They were all released on bond. Several weeks later, an angry Judge Vernor closed down the Bradshaw home by court order, placing restraining orders on the whole family and barring them from occupying the residence. County Attorney Floyd Green called the farm a "public menace and a gathering place for the county's criminal element." Two weeks after that action, a financial institution to which old Jim Bradshaw had mortgaged the home called in the note, repossessing the property. Rema and her attorney counter sued on both actions, but the court ruled against her. The property was soon sold to an area farmer. It seems that justly or not, the bankers finally got their revenge on the Bradshaws.

After this event, "Skeet," and several other family members got out of Dodge, joining thousands of fellow Oklahomans on the vast Okie migration to California. They settled near the town of Dixon, "Skeet" living with a cousin. Rema and her bunch moved to nearby Webber Falls, Oklahoma.

On July 5, 1937, Rema Deetjen was arrested in connection with the butcher-knife slaying of an eighteen-year-old Webber Falls girl. The victim was identified as Bernice

Part of the "Okie" migration to California. Photo courtesy of the National Archives Digital Collection.

Krammer, a waitress employed at the Ideal Café located in downtown Webber Falls and owned by Dr. Cecil Bryan and Blanche Cotner, sister of outlaw Charlie Cotner. Miss Krammer had been an employee there about four weeks.

While celebrating Independence Day, Deetjen, Krammer, and two men, Ernest Barnes and Melton Burk, had attended a drinking party at the Café. The four partygoers had left the restaurant around midnight after the owners, Cotner and Bryan, had ordered the four out of the café and locked the door behind them.

The partygoers moved their festivities to the banks of the nearby Arkansas River. Sometime during the night, the two women started calling each other names. The argument soon turned into a hair-pulling contest. It was never determined who started the fuss. The two men separated the females, attempting to calm the situation. The two couples left the river, returning to the café about 7 a.m. Shortly after the group's arrival back to the eatery, the two

Photo depicts the streets of Webber Falls around 1940. The Ideal Café where Rema Deetjen killed Bernice Krammer is pictured here as Barney's Place. The spot where Ford and Skeet shot the Black men is under the Mobile gas sign. Photo courtesy of the Webbers Falls Historical Society and Museum

women went at it again, pulling hair and attempting to scratch one another's eyes out. By most accounts, Rema retreated towards the rear of the café, when suddenly Blanche Cotner attacked the young woman.

When police questioned Dr. Cecil Bryan, he told officers he had heard a commotion coming from the front of the café. After walking from the rear of the building to the front, he saw Blanche Cotner and the young waitress fighting near the counter. Cotner had hold of Krammer by the hair and was bopping her over the head with a pop bottle. On the floor near the front counter police found numerous broken pop bottles, but were never able to establish how Cotner got involved in the fight with Krammer. Bryan also stated that after Blanche and Krammer had been fighting a short while, Rema Deetjen came from the kitchen with a butcher knife in her hand, which she plunged into the young woman's breast.

Muskogee County Deputy Trevor Wilma, who was driving down the main street of Webber Falls, noticed a crowd at the café and stopped to investigate. The town

The Ideal Café today. Photo by Naomi Morgan

constable, Fred Brimage, soon joined him with another deputy, W. R. Beavers. The trio began questioning several members of the crowd gathered outside the resturant. Most of them had heard screaming coming from the café.

It soon came to light that although there were four men in the business when the assault took place, none attempted to separate the fighting women during the attacks. The weapon, with bloodstains on the blade, was found in the back room of the café under a deer hide. Burke, one of the men present during the assault, stated he had made the knife while in prison.

The body of Miss Krammer was found lying on the floor behind the counter; there were bloodstains on the counter, stools, and floor. The officers learned from the four witnesses that Krammer was behind the counter and Cotner was in front when the stabbing occurred. All involved were arrested and taken to the Muskogee County jail. Murder charges were filed against Blanche Cotner and Rema Deetjen the following day. Bert Davis, an employee

Muskogee City Police Department with Sheriff Tom Jordan and staff shortly after his election. Photo courtesy of the Muskogee-Phoenix

at the café, and Dr. Bryan were released the next day after signing affidavits naming Rema as the killer. The two women's companions, Burke and Barnes, were held in jail on suspicion, but both had been too drunk on the morning of the killing to be of any help to investigators.

Newly elected Muskogee County Sheriff Tom Jordan and his deputies raided five businesses in downtown Webber Falls that evening. They seized numerous illegal slot machines and gaming devices from several of these businesses including Dr. Bryan's Ideal Café where the murder had taken place.

On July 7, eighteen-year-old Bernice Krammer was buried after a short graveyard service at the Gore Cemetery in a plain pine box. She lies in an unmarked grave.

On July 17, Blanche Cotner was released on $5,000 bond after a habeas corpus hearing. Her attorney, Phil Oldman, sought the release of his client contending there was not sufficient evidence to hold her. Oldman claimed in his argument before Judge E. V. Vernor that evidence showed Rema Deetjen had done the stabbing, adding his client had withdrawn from the fight before the fatal attack and she was not responsible for the acts of Rema Deetjen. The County Attorney, J. F. Beavers, protested Cotner's release on bond. He stated that she had stuck her nose into the two women's fight and

Sheriff Tom Jordan. Photo courtesy of the Muskogee County Sheriff Department

attacked Miss Krammer. He also stated that the physical evidence showed the victim was severely beaten about the head before she was stabbed. Witnesses said the cuts and bruises on Krammer's head were not inflicted on her in her earlier fight with Deetjen, but caused by Cotner's later assaults. Beavers also claimed he could prove Krammer was killed by Deetjen only because she was unable to defend herself while being held by Cotner. Two witnesses testified that Cotner and Krammer were still fighting when Rema stabbed her. In another legal motion, Cotner's attorney was able to convince the Judge to separate his client's trial from Deetjen's.

The trial of Rema Deetjan for the murder of Bernice Krammer began on February 15, 1938. Numerous witnesses were called for the prosecution including the coroner who testified that the knife in question had severed Krammer's aorta killing her very quickly. Rema told a completely different tale than Cotner or Bryan had presented. She claimed she was walking towards the rear of the cafe to fetch her purse, in which she kept a pistol, when she heard Miss Krammer scream and hit the floor. She denied she had stabbed anyone. She did admit she had been fighting with the young woman at the riverbank. When the prosecutor showed her the bloodstained butcher knife she looked at it unflinchingly and stated she had never seen it before.

The jury came back, after deliberating for more than six hours, with a verdict of guilty of first-degree manslaughter on February 18, 1938. The Judge sentenced her to five years at the Oklahoma State Prison. She became prisoner # 37426. The charges were dropped against Blanche Cotner, who went back to work at the café. She later served as Dr. Bryan's assistant in his practice in nearby Vian for many years.

With Rema's imprisonment and the loss of the family farm, the family split up and blew to the four winds. However, contrary to the popular notion, the sins of the fathers don't always pass on to the sons. The next several generations of descendents of the Cookson Hills gang pro-

Rema Deetjen (left) and Blanche Cotner (right) shortly after their arrest for the murder of eighteen year old Bernice Krammer. The two women are shown with Deputy Sheriff Paul Hinson leaving the Muskogee City Jail. Photo courtesy of Muskogee Times-Democrat.

duced collage professors, high school teachers, successful ranchers, preachers, and a host of honest hard working folk.

Chapter 12

Epilogue

With the building and paving of highways 82 and 17, which were ironically built partially by convict labor, the Cooksons became far less inaccessible. However, even more of a change came about in the latter 1940s with the construction of the Ten Killer Dam, which flooded the Illinois River. Sportsmen and tourists began crowding into the hills, forcing the bandit element to seek out other hideaways. Resorts and parks dot the area today. With the influx of new people, most of the natives have lost their suspicion of outsiders. Actually, the folks you meet in the Cooksons today are as open and friendly as anywhere else.

A modern view of the Site of the Susie Sharp killing. Photo by Naomi Morgan.

The old village of Cookson is underwater; the Corps of Engineers moved the existing buildings to higher ground in 1951 when the site was flooded. Nothing marks the spot where two lawmen and an outlaw lost their lives in the bloody shootout near Standing Rock; it's just a bend in the road. About five miles across the lake is a small grove of oak trees in the middle of a cow pasture where four other men were killed in the second bloody shootout the following day. "Kye" Carlile's relatives still own the land where the shootout took place.

The site of the Susie Sharp murder is now part of Camp Gruber, an Oklahoma National Guard base. That section of the old highway where the crime occurred has been abandoned and the area is now grown up and gone back to nature.

Although the Hills have become more passive nowadays, like the rest of the country, there's still too much violent crime there. In many remote sections, marijuana and methamphetamine is grown or produced. Its rumored there's always a whiskey still or two operating deep in the Hills. It is a place of many tales; stories told about buried outlaw loot or folks seeing the ghosts of Ned Christie. The Cooksons have an aura of duality, one that's mysterious, dark and dangerous and another that's of endless beauty. But, for all it's woes and bloody history over the years, the scenic country and the down-to-earth people there make it not only one of the most beautiful spots on earth, but a downright fascinating place.

A couple of miles west of present day Pin Hook Corners, Oklahoma, lays the site of the old Bradshaw home and cemetery. Only an abandoned well and a few foundation stones remain of the farm. If you follow a rough road that runs nearby into a valley a quarter mile distant, you will observe a grove of trees surrounded by a rusted barbed wire fence. Inside the fence, you can see about a dozen native stone rocks and a few rusted funeral home plaques that mark the final resting place of numerous Bradshaws and their kin. There are few names to see on these markers in this grown-up, weed-chocked plot. Many people who have lived their whole lives in the area know nothing of its existence. The last person was buried there in 1951. It now is surrounded by a cow pasture and is on private property.

The near fogotten, overgrown jungle where Ford Bradshaw is buried stands in marked contrast to the rolling, green, well-manicured lawns of the cemetery where Susie Sharp is resting. Who knows, maybe that's what they call "Karma," or a strange kind of justice.

For those that are curious about what became of the other characters noted in this book. I've listed many of their fates, as well as research could disclose.

****

The grave of Susie Sharp. Photo by Naomi Morgan

Grave of Ford Bradshaw. Photo by Naomi Morgan

The lawmen and victims:

V. S. CANNON: The nemesis of the Cookson Hills gang left his job as Muskogee County Sheriff in 1935. He was appointed chief of police in the city of Muskogee in 1938. The old crime-fighter next ran for and won election to the position of Mayor of Haskell, Oklahoma, in the 1940s. He was later elected to several terms as a Muskogee County Commissioner. He died in 1960, and is buried in Haskell.

The grave of V. S. Cannon. Photo by Naomi Morgan

******

RAYMOND DRAKE: Shot and severely wounded at the Bradshaw farm by Carl Janaway in 1936, he left the Sequoyah county sheriff's office later that year. He attended the first Oklahoma Highway Patrol school in 1938, and served as a state trooper until 1940. He returned to his farm, near Sallisaw, where he successfully raised blooded horses and Angus and Hereford cattle for the remainder of his life. He died on January 9, 1968.

******

BEN BOLTON: The chief of detectives of the Muskogee Police Department, who helped investigate the Susie Sharp murder, died a violent death. Bolton was killed in a jailbreak that occurred at the Muskogee City jail on December 3, 1935, involving members of the notorious O'Malley gang. He is buried in Muskogee's Green Hill cemetery.

The grave of Ben Bolton. Photo by Naomi Morgan

******

TOM JORDAN: The Muskogee County sheriff during Rema Deetjen's trial went on to serve four terms as Sheriff. In 1935, he led the posse that captured members of the O'Malley gang. He left the Sheriff's office in 1947. He later joined the Muskogee City Police Department in 1955. He died of a heart attack in 1956, at the age of fifty-three. He is buried at Memorial Park Cemetery in Muskogee, Oklahoma.

****

ED CORBIN: The Muskogee chief of police during the heyday of the Cookson gang, and a participant in the 1932 manhunt and ensuing shoot-outs, died of a heart attack in 1939. He was best known for his investigation of the 1930 Severs Hotel murders, which also made national headlines. Corbin rests in Muskogee's Green Hill Cemetery.

******

MARK LAIRMORE: One of the two Okmulgee lawmen who arrested and later transported Wilber Underhill to prison and had participated in the raid to apprehend the Eno brothers in Tulsa, went on to have a legendary career. In 1930, he left Okmulgee to work as a detective in the Tulsa Police Department. He survived many gunfights in his career, including a 1930 gun dual with bandits who had robbed the Bank of Coweta, Oklahoma. The trio led police on a high-speed chase that involved dozens of officers from five counties. It ended with Lairmore wound-

Mark Lairmore (holding gun) with other officers and bank robber of the Coweta bank. Photo courtesy of the Tulsa World and John Lairmore, son

ing all three outlaws. During his career, he was wounded three times and shot nine men in the line of duty. He was also the chief instructor at the Tulsa Police Department gun range. He wrote several classic articles on gun fighting for the department's monthly magazine. He died of a heart attack on the job in 1939. He is buried at the Okmulgee City Cemetery. His lifelong pal, ex-Okmulgee County Sheriff John Russell, went on to serve as the warden of one the state's prison farms. He passed on in 1977 and rests only a few feet from Lairmore's grave. They were a pair of true old-time frontier gunfighters.

******

GROVER BISHOP: He retired from police work in the 1940s. At the time of his retirement from law enforcement, he held a dubious record that will likely never be broken, of having killed fourteen men in the line of duty. This is more than any lawman in modern (1920 on) times in Oklahoma. He was a legend in the hills, where he was beloved by some and hated by others. Bishop died in March of 1980; he was 85 years old.

****

ROBERT LEDBETTER: Sheriff Cannon's undersheriff died in California in the 1960s.

******

JOHN "MARSH" CORGAN: Sheriff Cannon's hard-boiled, chief night deputy, was appointed   Muskogee's chief of police in 1935. In December of that year he was involved in the jailbreak at the city jail that resulted in the death of Detective Ben Bolton. Corgan responded by shooting and killing one of his assassins. In mid-1936, he lost his Chiefs position due to city politics. Corgan reportedly became despondent over the loss of his position and was suffering from ill health. His death by suicide at the age of forty-one on September 4, 1936, was a tragic loss for area law enforcement. He had been a legendary and fearless warrior in the war on crime. He was interred at Muskogee's Green Hill cemetery.

The grave of Marsh Corgan. Photo by Naomi Morgan

****

CASH RUSS: The Muskogee County Deputy Sheriff who identified the freshly killed Ford Bradshaw, died in 1973 in Muskogee at the age of 86.

****

JIM STORMONT: The Sheriff of Okmulgee County who pursued the Cookson Gang for several years, and helped capture the Eno brothers, quit law enforcement in the mid-30s and took up farming. He passed away in 1962 and is buried in Okemah, Oklahoma.

****

MAJOR WINT SMITH: The head of the Kansas State Police at the time of the gang's heyday, and a participant in the big Cookson raid, retired from law enforcement and later served as a US Congressman from his home state. He died in Jewell, Kansas, in 1973.

****

PRENTENCE MADDUX: One of the Sebastion County deputies present when Bradshaw was killed and a participant in the manhunt for Carl Janaway, died in Arkansas in 1960.

******

ELIAS SHARP: The husband of murder victim Susie Sharp died in 1966 and is buried next to his wife at Muskogee's Green Hill Cemetery. Their son, Owen Sharp, who was driving the car carrying his family that fateful night in 1932, passed on in 1967 and is buried near Braggs.

The grave of Elias Sharp. Photo by Naomi Morgan

****

RAY CRINKLAW: The sure-shot national guardsman died in Texas in 1959.

****

The Outlaws, Associates, and Family members:

CARL JANAWAY: The so-called "Terror of the Ozarks," was finally apprehended in St. Louis, Missouri and sentenced to federal prison. He served five years in Alcatraz, where he was "gofer" for fellow inmate Al Capone. He contracted TB and was transferred to the Federal Medical facility in Springfield, Missouri, in 1942. After serving nearly three years there in the prison hospital, he was released from Federal custody in 1944. Okla-

Carl Janaway. Photo courtesy of the Twin Territories Publications

homa authorities were waiting for him on the courthouse steps. He was hauled to Sallisaw to stand trial for the attempted murder of Deputy Raymond Drake. He was found guilty and sentenced to a ten-year term in the Oklahoma State Prison. After his release from the pen, he took up residence in Tahlequah, Oklahoma. The old bandit became a town character, telling tales of his adventures to all who would listen for many years. He died there in at the age of 94 at a local nursing home. He is buried in the city cemetery.

******

ROBERT TROLLINGER: Plead guilty on March 19,1934, to his participation in the robbery of the First National Bank of York, Nebraska and was sentenced to ten years at the Nebraska State Penitentiary. At his sentencing he remarked to reporters, he intended on "taking the rap and going straight" He was paroled from Prison on February 1,1941. Fortunately for him the states of Oklahoma and Kansas had dropped their hold orders on the bandit and did not attempt to prosecute him for his suspected crimes in the respective states. He died on November 21,1963 and was buried in the little cemetery in Barber, Oklahoma.

******

LUTHER JOLLIFF: He was released from federal prison after serving half a year and was on probation for a time. He died in 1950 and is buried in the Miller Cemetery in Cherokee County, Oklahoma.

******

THE ENO BROTHERS: Both served their time in the Kansas State Prison in Lansing and were paroled in the 1950s. Clarence was paroled on December 31,1953, and Otis on June 2,1954. The states of Oklahoma and Nebraska had by that time

Clarence Eno. Photo courtesy of Morton-James Library, Nebraska City, NE.

dropped their holds on the two bandits. After their release, they were lost in the mists of history. Otis' wife and Ford Bradshaw's sister, Clara "Gypsy" Eno, died in the 1980s and is buried in McAlester, Oklahoma.

******

ED DAVIS: One of Underhill's fellow Kansas prison escapees who robbed several banks with Wilber fled to California in late 1933. He was involved in a crime spree there, and was captured and sentenced to a term in the California State Prison on June 22, 1934. In September of 1937, he and several other inmates were involved in a failed escape attempt in which a guard and the Warden were killed. He

The capture of Ed Davis. Photo courtesy of the Muskogee-Times

was convicted along with the others of first-degree murder. Davis was put to death in the gas chamber in San Quentin, on December 16, 1938.

******

CHARLIE COTNER: Cotner managed to get his sentence reduced in 1951, and was paroled from the Kansas Prison in February 1952. The story told around Vian is that he was freed because he donated the cornea from one of his eyes to a small child suffering from a rare eye disease. According to Kansas prison authorities; his parole effort was given a great deal of assistance from several Vian businessmen, including a local banker. Ironically, after his release, Cotner did land a job working for the Bank of Vian, the same institution he had allegedly robbed, collecting overdue payments on farm loans. He was later employed at a horse racing track in Sallisaw. From all accounts, after his release from prison Cotner was a reformed man. He was known in later life as a kindly fellow, who volunteered his time at the Senior Citizens Center. He was extremely well liked and respected in the community. An old-time resident commented that Cotner once made the statement to him that he wished he had gotten a better start in life. It appears that he may have had a bad start, but by all indications, he ended it well. Charlie Cotner died in 1983 and was buried at the Vian Cemetery next to his brother, Hunter, who passed on in 1973, and his sister Blanche.

The graves of Charlie, Hunter, and Blanche Cotner. Photos by Naomi Morgan.

THOMAS "SKEET" BRADSHAW: He lived with relatives in California for several years, employed as a restaurant worker. He eventually got his own place near Vacaville. Bradshaw and his wife soon separated. He became a drifter and his family eventually lost touch with him. Perhaps he was trying to distance himself from the curse of self-destructiveness his family displayed. It is known that he was plagued the rest of his life by the ill effects of tuberculosis, alcoholism and near blindness. He died near Sacramento in the mid-1960s.

******

REMA BRADSHAW: Ford's sister was paroled back to society on October 7, 1939. According to family members, she remarried and made her home in McAlester for the rest of her life. The only public record of her after that is her death notice. She died in 1965 and is buried in McAlester's Catholic Cemetery.

******

"BOOTS" MOODY: The ultimate star-struck 1930s gangster moll was married and died in Oklahoma in the latter 1970s. What stories she could have told!

******

MOUNT COOKSON: The legendary old-time Cookson Hills bandit and sometime associate of the Bradshaw Gang, who started his career on horseback, was paroled from the Arkansas State Prison in 1940. After his release he told a friend he had enough of chopping cotton in Arkansas and intended on going straight. He died in 1953 and is buried in Tulsa, Oklahoma.

Mount Cookson grave. Photo by Naomi Morgan.

******

HAZEL HUDSON UNDERHILL: Wilber Underhill's widow remarried and moved to California. She died there on March 12,1979. Hazel had outlived five husbands. Her body was cremated then shipped back to Childers, Oklahoma where her ashes were buried next to the grave of her first husband, who had been killed by lawmen in 1923, while robbing a store near Coffeeville, Kansas.

"KAISER" BILL GOODMAN: The elderly associate of the Cookson Hills Gang who robbed his first bank when the rest of the gang was still wearing three cornered pants, met his Waterloo shortly after he and two partners robbed the Bank of Ketchum, Oklahoma on July 12, 1934. While making their getaway, the trio ran headlong into a posse led by Craig County Sheriff John York. All three bandits as well as a banker the trio had taken hostage were killed in the ensuing gunfight.

****

JIM BENGE: He was released from the Oklahoma State Prison in 1949 and received a full pardon from Governor Raymond Gary on December 18, 1958. On the morning of January 11,1959, Benge's badly beaten body was found by a pair of passersby lying in a snow covered ditch next to Highway 62, midway between Haskell and Boynton, Oklahoma. The county coroner ruled his death a homicide, caused by repeated blows to the back of the head with a blunt instrument. Sheriff Bill Vinzant commented, "Benge was apparently killed elsewhere and moved to the spot he was found." Robbery was assigned as the motive for the crime. Investigators had no suspects in the case and Benge's murder is still to this day unsolved. The old bandit was laid to rest at Greenleaf Cemetery in Cherokee County on January 16, 1959. With his death, all five suspects in the Susie Sharp slaying had met violent ends.

Cookson Hills Gang Robberies

1) October 7, 1931: First National Bank of Springdale, Arkansas robbed of $5,100. Suspects were: K. Carlile, R. Trollinger, and J. Benge.

2) August 1932: Citizens Security Bank of Bixby, Oklahoma, robbed of $1,000. Suspects were: K. Carlile, T. Love, Van Ratliff, R. Trollinger, F. Bradshaw, Eddy "Newt" Clanton, Fred Barker and J. Benge.

3) September 27,1932: Bank of Vian, Oklahoma, robbed of $6,000: suspects were F. Bradshaw, C. Cotner, S. Bradshaw, and E. Clanton.

4) November 7, 1932: American National Bank of Henryetta, Oklahoma, robbed of $12,000. Suspects were: F. Bradshaw, E. Clanton, and J. Benge.

5) February 1, 1933: Toll road robberies, Webber Falls, Oklahoma, the take was around $1,000. Suspects were: J. Benge, E. Clanton, and others.

6) February 27, 1933 The State Bank of Chetopa, Kansas, robbed of $1,300. Suspects were: S. Bradshaw and others.

7) May 31,1933 Bank of Chelsea, Oklahoma, robbed of $2,800. Suspects were: W. Underhill, Clarence and Otis Eno, E. Clanton and others.

8) September 20, 1933   First National Bank of York, Nebraska, robbed of $9,000. Suspects were: F. Bradshaw, C. Dotson, J. Harris, and R. Trollinger.

9) September 22, 1933   Peoples National Bank of Stuttgart, Arkansas, robbed of $1,000. Suspects were: W. Underhill, E. Davis, and C. Cotner.

10) October 9, 1933   American National Bank of Baxter Springs, Kansas, robbed of $3,000. Suspects were: F. Bradshaw, C. Cotner, C. Eno, E. Clanton, R. Trollinger and W. Underhill

11) October 9, 1933   Bank of Tyron, Oklahoma, robbed of $550. Suspects were: W. Underhill, and E. Davis

12) October 11,1933   International Bank of Haskell, Oklahoma, robbed of $1,000. Suspects were: W. Underhill, F. Bradshaw, C. Dotson, E. Clanton, or E. Davis.

13) October 24,1933   Merchants National Bank of Nebraska City, Nebraska, robbed of $6,135. Suspects were: Clarence and Otis Eno, C. Cotner, and Newt Clanton.

14) October 30,1933   National Bank of Galena, Kansas, robbed of $3,000. Suspects were: C. Cotner, F. Bradshaw, E. Clanton, and C. Eno.

15) November 2,1933   Citizens National Bank of Okmulgee, Oklahoma, robbed of $14,000. Suspects were: W. Underhill, F. Bradshaw, C. Eno, E. Clanton, and C. Cotner.

16) December 11,1933   First National Bank of Harrah, Oklahoma, unsuccessful robbery. Suspects were: W. Underhill, H. Nash, E. Inman, and R. Roe.

17) December 22,1933   First National Bank of Syracuse, Nebraska, robbed of $1,500. Suspects were: C. Eno, F. Bradshaw, R. Trollinger, and E. Clanton.

18) December 30,1933   National Bank of Mansfield, Arkansas, robbed of $1,700. Suspects were: M. Cookson, R. Trollinger, F. Bradshaw, "Kaiser" Bill Goodman

19) January 25, 1934   Bank of Wellington, Kansas, robbed of $4,000. Suspects were: C. Eno F. Bradshaw, O. Eno, and J. White.

20) February 24,1934   National Bank of Galena, Kansas, robbed of $7,100. Suspects were: C. Cotner, F. Bradshaw, S. Moody, and others.

21) 1933-1934   Banks of Windom, Honeywell, Weir, and Leroy, Kansas, Red Cloud and Kearney, Nebraska, Midland, Leslie, and Gravette, Arkansas, and seven others, robbed or burglarized in this time-period. Suspects were: C. Cotner, H. Cotner, The Eno brothers, "Newt" Clanton, G. R. Wright, E. Bass, F. Bradshaw, R. Trollinger, M. Cookson, E. Brophey, J. W. McAtee, F. Downey "Kaiser" Bill Goodman, "Bullet" Roland, "Kip" Harback, and others, who were all members or associates of Cookson Hills Gang.

Bibliography and Sources

Books

The Sequoyah County Historical Society (1976). *The History of Sequoyah County, 1828-1975.*

Allen, Eric (1974) *Crossfire in the Cooksons.* Hoffman Publishing

Okmulgee Historical Society (1985). *Okmulgee County History.* Tulsa, Oklahoma Historical Enterprises Inc.

Wallis, Michael (1992) *Pretty Boy: The Life and Times of Charles Arthur Floyd.* New York St. Martin's Press

Louderback, Lew (1968) *The Bad Ones: Gangsters of the '30s and Their Molls.* Fawcett.

Edge, L. L (1981) *Run The Cat Roads*, New York Dembner

Foreman, Grant (1940) *Fort Gibson, A Short Brief History,* Muskogee, Oklahoma Hoffman

Winter, Robert (2000) *Mean Men: The Sons Of Ma Barker*, Danbury, Connecticut, Rutledge

Payne, Betty, and Oscar (1954) *History of the old Dwight Presbyterian Mission*, Tulsa, Oklahoma, Dwight Presbyterian Mission

Kellner, Esther (1971) *Moonshine: It's History and Folklore*, New York, Bobbs-Merrill

Hiram, Juliana (1992) *History of Braggs*, Muskogee, Oklahoma, Private Printing

English, Billie and Calhoun, Sharon (1989). *Oklahoma Heritage*, Oklahoma City Oklahoma, Holt, Calhoun, Clark & Quaid

Hendrickson, Kenneth (1983). *Hard Times in Oklahoma, The Depression Years*, Oklahoma Historical Society

West, C.W (1976) *Muskogee, From Statehood to Pearl Harbor*, Muskogee Publishing

Etter, James Marion (1996) *Ghost-Town Tales Of Oklahoma: Unforgettable Stories Of Nearly Forgotten Places*, Stillwater, Oklahoma, New Forums Press.

Foreman, Grant (1942) *A History of Oklahoma*, Norman, Oklahoma, University of Oklahoma Press.

Horan, James D (1957) *The Desperate Years*, New York, Bonanza.

Shirley, Glenn (1978) *West of Hells Fringes*, Norman, Oklahoma, University of Oklahoma Press.

Helmer, Wm., Mattix. Rick (1998) *Public Enemies America's Criminal Past*, NY, Checkmark Books.

Articles and Periodicals:

Koch, Mike "The Tri State Terror, The saga of Wilber Underhill in Oklahoma." *Oklahombres Quarterly*, four-part series, 1994.

Mattix, Rick and Helmer, William J "Evolution of an Outlaw Band, The making of the Barker-Karpis Gang." *Oklahombres Quarterly*, two-part series, 1995.

West, Dub, Interview with Carl Janaway, Muskogee Publishing, Oklahoma, (1990).

Newspapers

Nearly 300 articles were consulted from the following newspapers:

Tulsa World Tulsa, Oklahoma, 1931-35.

Okmulgee Daily Times, Okmulgee, Oklahoma, 1931-34.

Muskogee Daily Phoenix, Muskogee, Oklahoma, 1920-45.

Muskogee Times-Democrat, Muskogee, Oklahoma, 1920-1945.

The Daily Oklahoman, Oklahoma City, Oklahoma, 1932-35.

Tahlequah Citizen, Tahlequah, Oklahoma, 1923-1934

Sallisaw Democrat-American, Sallisaw, Oklahoma 1930-45.

Vian Chief, Vian, Oklahoma, 1927-1945.

Joplin Globe, Joplin, Missouri, 1932-35.

Henryetta Daily Free Lance, Henryetta, Oklahoma, 1931-34.

Morris News, Morris, Oklahoma, 1931-34.

Oklahoma Legend, Tahlequah, Oklahoma, 2001.

Sapulpa Herald, Sapulpa, Oklahoma, 1932-35.

Galena Times, Galena, Kansas, 1933-35.

McAlester News Capital, McAlester, Oklahoma, 1928-45.

Haskell News, Haskell, Oklahoma, 1932-34.

Vian-Tenkiller News, Vian, Oklahoma 1996.

Claremore Daily Progress, Claremore, Oklahoma, 1931-1935.

Bristow News, Bristow, Oklahoma, 1932-35.

Vinita Leader, Vinita, Oklahoma, 1932-35.

The News-Press, Nebraska City, Nebraska.

York News-Times, York, Nebraska.

Springfield News-Leader, Springfield, Missouri.

Fayetteville Daily Democrat, Fayettville, Arkansas, 1931-34.

Sprindale News, Springdale, Arkansas, 1931-35.

Organizations

Appreciation is expressed to the following organizations for the use of their historical records, documents, microfilm, and archives:

Nebraska Department of Corrections

Oklahoma Department of Corrections

Kansas Department of Corrections

Arkansas Department of Corrections

Muskogee County District Court Clerk's office, Muskogee, Oklahoma

Sequoyah County District Court Clerk's office, Sallisaw, Oklahoma

Craig County District Court Clerkís office, Vinita, Oklahoma

Muskogee County Sheriff's Department, Muskogee, Oklahoma

Craig County Sheriff's Department, Vinita, Oklahoma

Northeast State University Library, Tahlequah, Oklahoma

Muskogee Public Library, Muskogee, Oklahoma

Haskell Public Library, Haskell, Oklahoma

Okmulgee Public Library, Okmulgee, Oklahoma

Muldrow Public Library, Muldrow, Oklahoma

Sapulpa Public Library, Sapulpa, Oklahoma

Henryetta Public Library, Henryetta, Oklahoma

Fort Smith Public Library, Fort Smith, Arkansas

Missouri State Collage Library, Joplin, Missouri

Bristow Public Library, Bristow, Oklahoma

Galena Archives Library, Galena, Kansas

Joplin Public Library, Joplin, Missouri

Vinita Public Library Vinita, Oklahoma

Sallisaw Library Sallisaw, Oklahoma

Coffeyville Public Library, Coffeyville, Kansas

Fayetteville Public Library, Fayetteville, Arkansas

Morton-James Public Library, Nebraska City, Nebraska

Kilgore Memorial Library York, Nebraska, Stan Schulz

Webber Falls Historical Society, Webber Falls, Oklahoma

Sapulpa Historical Society Sapulpa, Oklahoma

Bixby Historical Society Bixby, Oklahoma

Henryetta Historical Society Henryetta, Oklahoma

Cherokee Nation Resource Center Tahlequah, Oklahoma

Baxter Springs Heritage Center Baxter Springs, Kansas

Three Rivers Museum Muskogee, Oklahoma

Special Titles available from New Forums Press
call 1-800-606-3766 or go to www.newforums.com to order!

Oklahoma Cowboy Cartoons
-by Daryl Talbot

Award-winning cartoonist Daryl Talbot returns with this collection of cartoons depicting the funny side of modern cowboyin'. If you've ever owned a horse or worked on a ranch (or wished you did), you'll get a kick out of this lighthearted look at ranchin' and ropin'.

1999 (ISBN: 1-58107-014-4; 64 pages, 5 1/2 x 8 1/2, soft cover) $ 7.95

Between Me & You & the Gatepost— Rural Expressions of Oklahoma
(2nd, enlarged edition)

-by Jim Etter, illustrated by Daryl Talbot

A new and bigger edition of this popular collection of homegrown expressions and euphemisms that have distinguished the speech of Oklahoma folks for a coon's age and may do so 'til the cows come home. Take the bull by the horns and buy this book, and you'll be grinnin' like a possum eatin' persimmons!

1999 (ISBN: 1-58107-015-2; 44 pages, 5 1/2 x 8 1/2, soft cover) $ 7.95

Hilarious History: The Funniest True Stories and Legends of Stillwater and Payne County
-by D. Earl Newsom

A collection of many true stories of the early days of Stillwater and Payne County that in retrospect are hilarious, although they often involved bitter controversies at the time: adultery, fist-fighting attorneys, bootlegging preachers, and preachers' bitter debates (and fist fights). Taken from contemporary newspaper accounts.

1999 (ISBN: 1-58107-016-0; 60 pages, 5 1/2 x 8 1/2, soft cover) $ 7.95

The Cherokee Strip—Its History & Grand Opening
–by D. Earl Newsom

The opening of the Cherokee Outlet, popularly known as the Cherokee Strip, on September 16, 1893, was one of the great spectacles of American history. Relive the excitement in this outstanding volume. Includes a history of the Cherokee Nation; the towns of Alma, Blackwell, Enid, Newkirk, Perry, Ponca City, and Woodward, along with the 101 Ranch. Illustrated with 160 historical photographs.

1992 (ISBN: 0-913507-27-X; 209 pages, 6 x 9 inch, soft cover)　　　　　**$13.95**

Ragged Edges: Unusual Rag-Time Compositions
–by John Wilson

Here is a true delight for those interested in early Oklahoma history. Ragtime was the music of the period of the land-run and early statehood , the music that inspired, entertained, and delighted the pioneer forefathers of Oklahoma! You will be tapping your feet to Professor Wilson's skillful rendering of Eli Green's Cake Walk, Mandy's Ragtime Waltz, The Watermelon Trust Slow Drag, and others. And, those who play the piano will certainly enjoy trying their fingers at these invigorating tunes. **Includes audio cassette.**

1998 (ISBN: 0-913507-98-0; 122 pages, 8 1/2 x 11, soft cover, lay-flat binding)　　　　**$25.00**

A Distant Flame: The Inspiring Story of Jack VanBebber's Quest for a World Olympic Title
–by Jack VanBebber as told to Julia VanBebber

The autobiography of a sickly and partially handicapped Oklahoma boy who developed his abilities to become an NCAA champion wrestler at Oklahoma A&M, win a 1932 Olympic Gold Medal, and eventually be known as one of the ten greatest amateur wrestlers of all times. A must for young readers and sports fans.

1992 (ISBN: 0-913507-26-1; 192 pages , 5 1/2 x 8 1/2, soft cover)　　　　**$13.95**

Unforgettable Stories of Nearly Forgotten Oklahoma Places!

Ghost-Town Tales of Oklahoma—Unforgettable Stories of Nearly Forgotten Places can be found in many book outlets throughout Oklahoma and much of the nation, or can be ordered direct from the publisher or through the author (when ordering from author, please specify if autographed copies are desired).

When ordering direct, please include a check or money order for $16.45, which includes book price of $13.95 plus shipping costs (Oklahoma residents should send $17.95, which also includes applicable sales tax).

For orders and inquiries from publisher: New Forums Press, Inc., PO Box 876, Stillwater, OK 74076 • Phone 1-800-606-3766 or go to our web site at www.newforums.com!

197

The Story of Exciting Payne County
– by D. Earl Newsom

A virtual encyclopedia of Payne County, its towns and villages, and its people since the 1889 land run. Included are detailed histories of the major towns (Stillwater, Cushing, Perkins, Yale, Glencoe, and Ripley), histories of the once thriving oil towns, brief histories of more than 20 villages that have virtually disappeared, maps, photos, lists of county officials, and dates of major events in every community. *1997 (ISBN: 0-913507-91-1; 272 pages, 8 1/2 x 11 inch, hard cover)* $29.95

Stillwater History - The Missing Links
-by D. Earl Newsom

Fascinating events, Stories and Pictures not included in Previous Books. D. Earl Newsom's final book dealing with Stillwater history and at his request a limited edition was published. The Madeline Webb Murder Trial, the Mathews Murder Case, the Ku Klux Klan, Stillwater's Movie Histories, "Doc" Whittenberg, the Ramsey Oilfield,Stories behind Street Names and Hotels, Taxis and Buses. *2000 (ISBN: 1-58107-027-6; 72 pages, 8 1/2 x 11 inch, soft cover)* $15.95

Claiming the Unassigned Lands
-by Clyde Shroyer

Mr. Shroyer has researched and gathered family information, backing it up with historical research to accomplish the task of telling his family story and their role in Oklahoma History. Recommended by the 1889er Society *2000 (ISBN: 1-58107-025-X, 390 pages, 5 1/2 x 8 1/2, soft cover)* $19.95

Remembrances of Sapulpa (Vol 1.)
–by Virginia Wolfe

Compiled from the author's weekly column for the *Sapulpa Daily Herald* celebrating Sapulpa's centennial, this first volume of a projected ten-volume series tells the story of Sapulpa's growth and development as seen through the eyes of many of its founding families and leading citizens. Liberally illustrated. A real nostalgia trip!

1998 (ISBN: 1-58107-010-1; 138 pages, 8 1/2 x 11 inch, soft cover)   **$25.00**

The First Generation—A Half Century of Pioneering in Perry, Oklahoma
-by Fred G. Beers

A glimpse at the earliest days of Perry, Oklahoma, and the Charles Machine Works, Inc., the manufacturer of Ditch Witch® equipment, through five decades from a bald, treeless prairie at the middle of the great land rush of 1893 to today's bustling, verdant community populated by picturesque descendants of hardy pioneer stock.

1991 (ISBN: 0-913507-22-9; 384 pages, 6 x 9, hard cover)   **$19.95**

Hiram and the Rattales
–written and illustrated by Joan Bartlett Brozek

A unique look at Oklahoma and American history as seen through the eyes of a special family of rats living in southern Oklahoma. Papa Rattale tells his children the stories of the great events of American history as handed down to him by his ancestors. A book that makes American and Oklahoma history come alive for the young and the young at heart.

1988 (ISBN: 1-913507-39-3; 90 pages, 5 1/2 x 8 1/2, soft cover)   **$ 7.95**

Y-O-U and The I-O-A Way
-by Lea Ann Donnelley Walker
and Richard Green

A chronicle of the Oklahoma Lions Boy's Ranch, its philosophy, and the Main and Donnelley families who founded it, told by the daughter of cofounder H.F. Donnelley. Liberally illustrated, including many facsimile documents. Proceeds from the sale go to support of future programs of the Ranch.

1998 (ISBN: 0-913507-90-3; 170 pages, 8 1/2 x 11, soft cover)   **$20.00**

Thunder in the Heartland – Parables from Oklahoma
-by Jim Marion Etter

Just as truth is often stranger than fiction, sometimes it takes a touch of fable to give a true story the luster of immortality. At least, this seems so with Oklahoma, where, except for monumental events like the 1995 Oklahoma City bombing, many significant moments in history have been largely forgotten. They have been left to sleep in the memories of a few and on microfilmed pages of yesteryear's newspapers, in obscure library books or in dusty court records.

Except for the one based on the bombing itself, the following stories, all of which are fiction inspired by fact, are an attempt to awaken a few of these happenings, circumstances and traditions that in fact *are* the Sooner State. Any similarity between some fictitious name and that of a real person, of course, is a flat accident.

Author Jim Etter has completed an excellent collection of compelling stories with which all Oklahomans can identify. A must for your reading pleasure!

2000 (ISBN: 0-58107-034-9; 214 pages, 5 1/2 x 8 1/2, soft cover)   **$14.95**